MEDITATION
for MOMS
and DADS

108 Tips for Mindful Parents and Caregivers

By Shana Smith, c. 2016
Illustrations by Grace Ohana Smith

ClearSky Publishing
San Clemente

Published by:

ClearSky Publishing
645 Camino de los Mares
Suite 108-276
San Clemente, CA 92673

Visit our website at www.ClearSkyPublishing.com

Book Design by Reyhana Ismail
Book Design by Scribe Freelance | www.scribefreelance.com

ISBN: 978-0-9965453-2-7
First Edition

Printed in the United States of America

For my family. And yours.

CONTENTS

Foreword

In his preface to the renowned collection of koans, the *Mumonkan* or *Gateless Gate*, Zen Master Mumon Ekai (1183-1260) cites an old saying: "Things that come in through the gate are not family treasures." Thus, at the outset of offering a series of koans—tools by which students of the Way might "knock at the gate" of their own true nature—Master Mumon points to the reality for which no gate can be found. This is the seeming paradox of the Dharma. That which we seek is as intimate and immediate as seeking itself. And yet, for those intent on awakening, seek we must!

The urgency to practice is the starting point for Shana Smith's *Meditation for Moms and Dads: 108 Tips for Mindful Parents and Caregivers.* Writing from the intersection of her own deeply-rooted meditation practice and her experience with a variety of spiritual traditions, Shana plunges into the endless demands and delights of daily life as a "Householder" and asks: Where else but *here* is the place of practice? At what time but *now* can a working parent, spouse, homemaker, and world-dweller engage in mindful living and cultivate a spiritual path?

In response, Shana takes up her own life as a living koan. With deft insight, disarming humor, and a wellspring of gratitude, she offers guidance and inspiration for practice in the context of family life—or for anyone caught in the swell of busyness that can swamp every good intention to *stop and see.* Her work is not intended as authoritative but rather as an invitation. Here, Mumon's ancient reference to the "family treasures" takes on an ironic twist. Family is precisely the context for realizing the treasure that no words can convey and no amount of practice can accomplish. Shana calls this uncompromisingly intimate treasure "Allness, Suchness." She notes the freedom that just one glimpse of this treasure can unleash. It is YOU from the beginning. How, then, can you see it?

One hundred eight is the number of prayer beads on a mala as well as the number of delusions to be seen through or stamped out in meditation practice.[1] The correspondence is fitting. Shana's 108 tips can be turned like beads in the hand, a breath counted, an emptying prayer; or they may wield a word that helps to cut through the delusive concepts and constructs that trap us in a false sense of separation and defend us against the very wisdom and compassion that is our birthright.

Beginning with a reframing of the Four Noble Truths, *Meditation for Moms and Dads* threads a Middle Way right through the ups and downs of everyday experience. The imperatives of daily life devoted to the care of children and family ring out: "Kaboom!" "Crash!" "Global warming?!" "Clean socks?!" Yet earnestly walking this Way, somehow, again and again, Grace prevails. Suffering becomes an impetus to practice and a portal to joy. Attachment gives way to acceptance. Fear dissolves into freedom. As Shana sees it, meditation, the root of the Way, is at once essential and rendered in flexibility. Mindfulness practice is everywhere available and sometimes astonishing in the simple shift it can bring.

Meditation for Moms and Dads offers a creative and readily accessible series of pointers for practice. Alongside this written offering, Shana and her husband Dan have shaped their lives to offer a dedicated place of practice for others. In 2010, they began hosting weekend retreats in their home on a beautiful and wild 108-acre nature preserve in Gainesville, Florida. Established meditation teachers were invited and the Gainesville Retreat Center was born. For the next four years, Shana and Dan ran the Center from afar, commuting back and forth from their working life in the Tampa Bay area to provide every level of support and to join in practice as much as possible. Their two young children, Grace Ohana and Benny, made multiple trips as well. The children thrived in this setting, a sign to Shana that the deep longing to devote her life to practice was not for herself alone.

---

[1] The sounding of the han or drum at the end of the day during Zen retreats (sesshin) intones the stamping out of 108 delusions. It has been said that if just one sound can truly be heard, one's practice is at an end. Then it can begin.

In 2013, Dan and Shana took the "leap of faith" and moved the family back to their home in Gainesville. Drawing on their experience hosting retreats and Dan's knowledge of architectural design and contracting, they used their savings to build a simple but functional retreat center. In January 2014, the new GRC opened and the first retreat was held.

When I first stepped into the new zendo of the GRC, almost two years ago now, a line of verse that found its way into the *Gateless Gate* came immediately to mind: "The radiance serenely illumines the whole vast universe."[2] Surely the dedication and loving intention that suffuses Shana's writing has something to do with this radiance. Still more direct is the vast translucent space, empty, the whole world shining; at once awaiting practice and complete from the start.

There is another timeless verse that presents itself when standing in the zendo that Shana and Dan built: "I don't know the reason why, but tears of gratitude fall from my eyes."[3] This gratitude goes beyond appreciation for the particulars of our lives, for needs met, for possessions, relationships, for earth, sun, and sky. It is the unknowing and unconditional gratitude that is the ground of practice. It is, as Shana suggests to Householders in search of a Spiritual path, the place to begin.

For moms and dads who would like to take up the invitation to practice—without waiting until the kids are grown, without waiting until the busyness ceases, without waiting: enter here and enjoy.

Palms together,

Valerie Keiun Forstman
Associate Zen Master, Sanbo Zen
Thanksgiving 2015

---

[2] See Case 39 of the *Mumonkan*. The line is from the enlightenment verse of Chōsetsu Shūsai.
[3] Anonymous Japanese verse. Translation by Ruben Habito Roshi.

Acknowledgements

Thank you to Valerie Forstman Roshi of the Maria Kannon Zen Center in Dallas, Texas, for her compassionate teachings, her presence, encouragement and guidance to continue "straight on" this path, and for the critical review of this book. To the Venerable Uda Eriyagama Dhammajiva of the Mitirigala Nissarana Vanaya Monastery in Sri Lanka, for his teachings and his recognition of Mindful Families. To Reverend Meredith Garmon of the UU Church in White Plains, New York, for introducing me to the formal and committed practice of Zen meditation. To Michael Singer of the Temple of the Universe in Alachua, Florida, for igniting and maintaining the fire of spirituality and "getting free" as the only true basis for my life. To ClearSky Publishing for seeing the potential in this book and the opportunity to work with your wonderful team. To my husband, Dan Smith, for his unwavering support, love, wisdom, and commitment to our shared journey together. To my mother, Debby Townsend, for her unconditional love and for being my first and continuing teacher. To the memory of my late father, Dr. Albert C. Smith, for introducing me to Oneness with his deep love of the ocean. To my sister, Nathan Strange, for our link deep and eternal; I love how we continue to grow up together. To my lifelong best friend, Emily Huang, for our living example of timeless, ageless connection. To my children and gurus, Grace Ohana and Benny Albert, for their brilliance, making this journey deeper and more meaningful than I could have ever imagined. To my other teachers along the Way. To my sangha, for our dance in the dharma, together.

"You are not the Giver of Love. You are not the Receiver of Love. You are Love."

Introduction

A few years ago, when I was several years into a solid meditation practice, I was invited to participate in a week-long sesshin (extended meditation retreat) at a prominent Zen Center. My daughter was four and I was very pregnant with my son, and as the sesshin was during a time that my son would be a newborn, it was not possible to attend. An established and well-intentioned meditation teacher told me it would be at least ten years before I could get back to a formal, consistent meditation practice, and that until that time, I would have to lessen, modify and change my practice until being able to return to the dedicated routine that had become near, dear, and something I could not live without. This did not "sit" well—if this path is right here, right now—if the True Self is within and instantly accessible, what is all this waiting for my kids to get bigger business?

The practice of mindfulness, achieved via meditation, is described by The Greater Good Science Center in Berkeley, California as "maintaining a moment-by-moment awareness of our thoughts, feelings, bodily sensations, and surrounding environment. Mindfulness also involves acceptance, meaning that we pay attention to our thoughts and feelings without judging them—without believing, for instance, that there's a 'right' or 'wrong' way to think or feel in a given moment. When we practice mindfulness, our thoughts tune into what we're sensing in the present moment rather than rehashing the past or imagining the future."[i]

Wouldn't meditation be essential for cultivating mindfulness during the experience of parenting, as well as support the development of mindful, compassionate children? If we are to fulfill our ultimate job as parents and effect compassion, peace, and loving kindness in this world, we need a way to maintain a dedicated meditation practice, and even feel warmly encouraged to begin one for the first time.

If you are reading this, it is likely that you too are smack in the middle of what is commonly called the "Householder" phase of life—a busy, busy, busy time largely consumed with caretaking, peanut butter and jelly sandwiches, a softening mid-line, a sagging bottom-line, sleep deprivation, house and vehicle maintenance, and work. It is the post-power Yogi/Zen student, pre-retired retreat attendee/Zen master phase, and is often all but dismissed in the Spiritual Seeker world save some token yoga classes at the gym. While meditation groups are available, there is rarely child care offered, and it is hard to pay a babysitter $60/week so you can go and sit with a bunch of people for a few hours. You try to do it yourself, whenever and wherever you can. And it's almost impossible... certainly not anything like what the "old you" was capable of, when there was some sense of space and potential in your daily life and goals. There is just too much to think about, manage, and do. In fact, many great gurus, masters, artists, scientists and other mad geniuses either forego or give up on this whole Householder phase entirely. And yet, in so many of us, the yearning exists, as it should, for the siren song of Spirit is irresistible.

Look at the definition of "Householder" as it stands: you are alive and you live in a house. For 98% of the world, that is in itself a miraculous gift. The house has electricity when you pay the bill, a roof that usually doesn't leak too much, and enough space for all of your stuff. And you have stuff. Sometimes way too much stuff. And you go to the grocery store and buy food. Lots and lots of food. Organic food. GMO-free food. Gluten-free food. Vegan food. Gourmet food. And you might have a garden to grow more food. And you go to other stores to buy processors and blenders and juicers for your food. And you go to other stores to buy clothes and housewares. And you have kids and/or other beings you steward, and they are probably alive and hopefully healthy, and if they are not, you have lots of resources to help you through. And you may or may not have a partner to help you take care of them and all of your stuff. I can think of about eight billion people who would give anything for the "Householder" scenario, and there was a time, before this scenario, that you probably would have given anything for it as well. So, there is absolutely no reason a Householder should not be an intent Spiritual Seeker, because any Householder in his or her right mind is full of Gratitude. Gratitude is one of the most basic tenets of Spirituality.

But stuff and children come with work and responsibility, and caregivers often feel that their "cup runneth empty." We caffeinate, we commiserate, we think really hard about things, we work hard and "do the best we can." We wake up more often tired than ecstatic. The siren song of spirituality beckons and we smile wanly, barely hearing it over the Disney movies and PBS Kids shows that sound track your current life, asking it to wait a little longer, while our minds spin and churn with how to best manage another day. In fact, the word "mindfulness" itself seems to be a paradox, as indeed our minds are very, very, full, and parents are prime models of the brilliance of the human mind to be able to calculate, pontificate, extrapolate, coordinate, and manage twelve or even twelve hundred things all at the same time. As Yoda might say: "Brilliant, you are. But run out it will, your access to the Force, if you do not know how to allow it to find you over and over again."

As our minds spin and churn, we cannot comprehend that that coveted spirit song, or the "Force" if you will, isn't far away. In fact, it's right there at the center of our being, enclosed in our hearts, yearning to burst open and flood our entire consciousness with presence, to fill our cups without end, to sustain us effortlessly, to break us out into song, if we see it, feel it, and allow it to be so.

To continue the sci-fi analogy, as Captain Jean-Luc Picard of "Star Trek, The Next Generation" so famously commands: "Make it so." Do not wait. There is another way besides hard work and suffering. It's called meditation. It requires a subtle yet deeply powerful shift in our long-conditioned patterns of thinking and relating to the world around us.

Meditation comes in many forms, from formal sitting on a zafu cushion to walking on the beach to picking up spilled Legos one by one off of the floor, to whatever form of prayer or ritual devotion you might do, to yoga to gardening. It is perhaps the most essential daily practice a parent will ever do, one which brings us home to the source of infinite

Love, and creates an environment inside that radiates outward to the benefit of everyone. Over time, and sometimes very quickly after you've launched this path of mindfulness and meditation, your cup will "runneth over." Not only will you find the "Force;" you will BE one.

Therefore, stubbornly, with two active, small-to-medium children and anywhere from two to twelve pets at any given time and two jobs and a house and a wonderful husband, I have refused to give up my very earnest and devoted meditation practice. However, I have discovered that it does need to be modified, and often with a good dose of humor. Talk about the ultimate lesson in non-attachment, as indeed the traditional ways of meditation and spiritual seeking sometimes just don't sync with the "Householder" scenario. Hence, this book—tried and true tips for all moms, dads, and caregivers—was born. "Meditation for Moms and Dads" is really for everyone, as life is our beloved path and we all care for and parent one another along the way. There are 108 tips from my own experiences, and real life stories from a diverse array of parents, grandparents, and caregivers from many different backgrounds who parent in many different ways.

Speaking of which, this book is not meant to be an advice resource on how to parent your children; that's your choice. It is simply an invitation to connect to this present moment—and now this one—and now this one—with a deep and ever-accessible love and awareness that starts within, based on ancient practices that really work. While you're doing it, children just happen to be a central part of your consciousness and are often in tow, providing ever-amazing opportunities to enrich your practice and live in total presence with them.

Have fun!

About Meditation

One internet search of the word "meditation" will bring up 132 million results. There will be references to insight meditation, concentration meditation, vipassana meditation, mindfulness meditation, transcendental meditation, loving-kindness meditation, science-based meditation, prayer-based meditation, guided meditation, benefits of meditation, the science behind meditation, the spiritual elements of meditation, Buddhist, Yogic, Christian, Jewish, Muslim, Native American, and Atheist meditation techniques, to name only a few. Tabloids and women's magazines will espouse meditation as the cure for headaches and cheating husbands, the source of psychic powers and the key to manifesting riches and glory. Definitions of the word "meditation" are likewise diverse. According to the Buddhist Centre, meditation is a "means of transforming the mind."[ii] Deepak Chopra describes meditation as "a way to get in the space between your thoughts." [iii] Yoga Journal refers to meditation as a "technique used for focusing the mind and observing ourselves in the present moment."[iv]

Out of curiosity, I posed the question "What is meditation?" to a pool of friends and colleagues and received over 100 different responses over a 24-hour period. Some responses referred to meditation as a time for focus and concentration, many said it was putting emphasis on the present moment, others described it as a way of getting to a place of deep peace, while still others referred to connecting with a Divine presence or force in the Universe. Some of the responses that are most salient to our goal—that is, to champion meditation as an essential and wonderful practice for parents—are listed below.

- Meditation is the disciplining of posture, breathing, and stilling the mind to rest in things just as they are. What a gift to be alive and have the opportunity to pursue this clarity, to awaken to our true nature. At the same time, our pursuit is itself the perfect expression of the very thing we seek. From the beginning, fully realized. (Valerie Forstman Roshi, Zen Teacher)

- I sit. Just the act of sitting quiets the mind. Watch my breath, softly. Willing to be with whatever shows itself. Not trying to do anything, not trying to change myself, not trying to make anything happen. Surrender. (Fern Williams, Mother of Four, Retired Nurse Practitioner)

- Calming the conscious mind enough to consciously connect to the subconscious mind. Or sometimes it's washing the dishes. (Dana Mbo'nsrh Gilmore, Mother)

- Being a busy mom with young children who works from home, meditation for me is like pushing the pause button of life, even if for a brief moment, to take a breath bringing my focus back into myself before I push the play button again. Meditation looks different depending on my day. Sometimes it's closing my eyes while I smell a flower, taking a bubble bath with candles, listening to a song while absorbing the lyrics, daydreaming, running, painting or other forms of creative expression, walks in nature or even just stepping outside to enjoy my yard, being at the ocean. Occasionally it's a more formal guided meditation. At the heart of any of them is a conscious effort to bring my energies back into my core to help ground me and reenergize myself. (Mychele Boardman, Mother of Four, Artist)

- "Taking the time to connect with all things around you while reaching an inner calmness or peace." (Loren Ellis Smyth, Mother of Two)

- "For me, it's turning off self-talk and turning on self-listening." (Carolyne Salt, Actor/Director)

- "Meditation is letting go of thoughts and allowing the mind's chatter to be still." (Radha Dainton, Mother of Two, chef)

- "I think meditation is a way to connect to the fundamental nature of things. For me, it has two forms. The first form is through activity of some sort and the ability to be focused and connected deeply to that activity. In this expression, I seek to merge with the activity and am not separate from it. The second form is the opposite–sitting. This expression is the attempt to settle the mind by allowing all thoughts and mental arisings to dissipate until nothing is left but core." (Ted Berry, Father, Businessman)

- It is total surrender to the present moment... a choice to let go of control and allow peace in every cell of your body. Surrender, allow, release, let go, breathe. These are beginnings. Beyond that is light... on a lot of different levels. (Bettina Makely, Artist, Musician)

- Meditation is concentrating on something like the breath or just a detail of one of the senses until the ego mind gets so bored it just goes to sleep and shuts up long enough for us to listen to the Source, Divinity, God, the Universe, whatever we want to call it—the Is-ness of Infinity! (Judi Cain, Mother of Two, Visual Artist)

- Forcing my brain and body to get back in sync with each other in order to calm the chaos that is my life. It gets rid of the feeling that my brain is in merry-go-round mode. (Betsy Jenkins, Audio Engineer, Shuttle Driver, Entrepreneur)

- Sitting with what is. Allowing time to be present to Source energy. (Dana Feldmeier, Nutrition Coach)

- Going to that place of peace in your mind where you're living only the moment and enjoying it fully. (Deborah Townsend, Mother and Grandmother of Two, Master Gardener, Artist)

- Aligning my consciousness with Love, the supreme source of love, the highest vibration transcendental to my human limitations. Reminding myself that I am a spiritual being having a human experience. Finding acceptance again and again as the door to lightness of being, as many times as I need to find it. (Sarah Thompson, Life Coach)

- To me, meditation is being very present in the moment, with a mind free of extraneous thought, whether engaged in a physical activity or in quiet receptive times—when the Pure Energy of Life flows through unimpeded by ego. (Trish Harding, Elementary School Teacher)

- What we call "meditation" includes a number of different practices, but these practices are all ways to train the mind. It is a useful, effective component in what you might consider a spiritual wellness program. If you want to be physically healthy and resilient, you might do different kinds of exercise that develop the body's ability to manage challenges skillfully. Likewise, you can train the mind so that it can handle spiritual challenges skillfully. (Morris Sekiyo Sullivan, Zen Master, Buddhist Minister)

- Meditation is becoming the universe within the self. (Tom Miller, Artist)

- Meditation is focusing on the present moment. It is coming into contact with what is and consciously expanding presence until ego is dissolved. Needless to say, this takes lots of practice and happens over and over because we constrict, lose contact with presence and allow ego to take over. (Lisa Litz, Musician, Vocalist, Mental Health Therapist)

- What is happening right now? What am I feeling? What am I thinking? What am I assuming? What am I holding on to? (John David Eriksen, Cellist)

- "Meditation is a specific moment of concentration; you can listen to your body or to nature and concentrate on the energy that is circulating/flowing." (Cecile Pantin, Mother of Two, Vocalist)

- "Meditation is something mommy and daddy love because it gives them peace and mindfulness and they can be careful, and I can too, like if daddy has a cup of coffee, don't come running to him." (Benny, First Grader)

- There are as many different answers to this question as there are meditators... because meditation is an intensely personal experience. (Charley Groth, Folk Musician)

What is clear from this inquiry, as Charley so aptly states, is that the question "What is meditation?" holds uniquely different answers for different people. It is a deeply personal and organic experience. Just as you can't ask the question: "What is parenting?" and expect to get the same answers from your pool of questionees, so it is for meditation, and that's why meditation is such a perfect partner to parenting. Because your meditation is not another's, it will compliment and transform the true experience of your own life and the journey will be all yours. Likewise, it will connect you organically and compassionately to those on their own paths, rising you out of the bubble of your individual being, needs, wants and judgments and up into the vast, all-inclusive universe where we all reside.

While no parenting experience is the same, we all need to know the basic foundation from which to work on how to effectively feed, clothe, educate, and care for our children, and the same goes for meditation. It is helpful to have some standard information on what meditation is and how to begin a practice.

As it is usually referred to as a "practice," many parents are deterred from the upstart since that very word often conjures up already saturated images of piano practice, soccer practice, play practice, and similar involvements which usually involve significant chauffeuring and financial outputs. Just as those types of practices make better musicians, better athletes, better performing artists, etc., thus paving the way to potential college scholarships and a lifetime of work, security, and recognition, your meditation practice will indeed make you a better meditator and provide you with more inner security, but not for competitive reasons. You will not strive to win a competition in how long you can sit on a cushion with hands in the most perfect mudra, without moving or making a sound. There will be no trophy bestowed to the busiest mom or dad with the quietest mind. The practice of meditation is a continuous re-learning and re-orienting of your perception. It's a releasing of longstanding habits of the mind. It's like learning how to saunter when you have always run, or learning how to speak a new language that offers more levels of expression than you ever thought possible. You have to first learn what to do and why it's important, and then do it regularly and diligently until it eventually becomes a part of you. Scholarships and recognition will become but ego-based shadows in the light of a new relationship with your more spacious mind, a relationship which bestows a fresh awareness and appreciation of the experience of Life as We Know It. In other words, the "We Know" part of Life as We Know It will change, or even disappear completely, to become simply "Life as It."

Thus comes the crux of this whole chapter: What IS it that you are doing regularly and diligently that is bestowing all of this fresh awareness and knowing? What is meditation? What is a meditation practice? How do you start, and how do you continue?

So What Is Meditation?

Despite 132 million variations on a theme, there are common elements that can distill meditation into a definition that reads something like this:

> *Meditation is the practice of using various techniques to cultivate a positive relationship with your mind, an intimacy with the present moment, and a connection to a greater awareness that yields transformational results both within and without.*

The benefits of this practice are indeed calmness and peace, compassion and kindness; certainly this is the case in the long run, with diligent and regular practice. But with this diligent and regular practice, the meditator often finds that each time they meditate, a still mind and a compassionate nature may or may not always ensue. Sometimes, it's quite the opposite: as we delve deeper into the inner world, as we face the realities of the good, the bad, and the ugly as we bravely face our true consciousness, longstanding mud gets stirred up. It must be stirred up and released in order for us to get clear. The Buddha himself preached that "purity of the mind" is our one true cause in this lifetime. Meditation means willingly, even earnestly, getting to and through our mud.

Since our existence in this lifetime is dependent on relationships of all sorts, there is perhaps no more meaningful relationship than the one you cultivate with your own mind. By definition, then, if we sit fully intent on making our mind stop, we have quashed our relationship with it. We've denied access to the "mud," or worse, pushed it down inside of us even deeper. Moreover, it would be an impossible task, an unreachable expectation, to think that one's mind can and should be quiet all the time, like an inappropriately loud child who must be shushed. Meditators have found great peace and stillness through their consistent practice, sure, but not because their minds are always still. Sometimes they are; sometimes they're not. A great benefit of this practice is that our minds will attain ever-increasing stillness over time. But as we will discuss next, we don't always want our mind to shut up. We need it to help us function and do things, like figure out how to pay the bills or counsel our emotionally struggling teenager. Most of all, meditation makes us aware that we are not our minds. There is a place that watches the mind—and that's the place we want to call "home." That is the place we work in synergy with the critical functions of our mind, without letting it take over.

Now, before I go on to the next question: How do I meditate? Let me clarify and reiterate this very important point. Your mind is not your enemy. In addition to not trying to push it away, it should be appreciated for the critical job it was meant to do. The mind, despite its bad rep, frequent unruliness, and muddiness, has an important function. It calculates, regulates, figures, and accounts for your basic needs. As such, those who meditate learn to honor that job, encourage it, and use the inherent vital skills of the brain to function in the world. What parent, who has to multitask and manage almost every aspect of their waking hours, would not be thankful for the key functionality that the mind bestows? How else can we make lunches, tutor math, change a diaper, conduct an online meeting and get dressed all at the same time? That's right folks: our brilliant multifunctioning mind makes it all possible. When I stop and contemplate the service of the mind from a parent's perspective, I want to put it up on my meditation altar, right next to the Buddha statuette and the mala beads, or at least give it a much-deserved bow.

So the mind's monkeyish tendencies hinder our path to liberation, and yet its abilities are indispensable to our basic functioning. How to approach this apparent duality in our meditation practice? In addition to generally and genuinely appreciating our mind as a critical step towards our relationship with it, the key to meditation is to learn to discriminate between these important quality functions versus the ego that tells us that we need to be scared, worried, anxious and attached—

the part that changes its own mind with a shift in the wind and drives us to high states of anxiety if we allow ourselves to be swept away with it. Meditation is getting to know the mind in all of its guts and glory, and to begin to identify oneself with the one—YOU—who is watching that mind. It's a beautiful relationship, that between the permanence of the Watcher and the impermanence of the ever-changing less functional aspects of the Mind, and one that will set you free.

So, with all of this in... er... mind, know that as a parent you will have a great time in meditation because you will likely get to know your mind, at any given time, in one of these three states, in order from least to most likely, from a parent's perspective:

1) STILL MIND. This state is very rare in the early stages, though is quite attainable with regular practice, and is not to be confused with the fact that you fell asleep while meditating.

2) MONKEY MIND. This type of mind activity is the one most talked about in meditation teachings. It means exactly what it sounds like: your mind is all over the place, jumping from one emotion and its reaction to the next, worrying, creating mountains out of anthills, thumping your chest, awfulizing, daydreaming, fantasizing, and carrying on. The instruction in dealing with this type of mind involves letting go—not getting swept up in reactivity, but rather noticing the feelings and thoughts as they come and go without judgement.

3) PARENT MIND. This type of mind activity is the one least talked about and most misunderstood, mainly because parenting and meditating have not, until now, been commonly recognized in the same sentence. It is the one most pertinent to this book and our practice. Because there is so much to do and manage as a parent, we have become masters of multitasking and details. We know that missing even one detail can be critical to the well-being of our children and the functioning of our household, and

as such our brain is entirely consumed with getting all of the details correctly figured out and managed. Meditation becomes an at times excruciating exercise in simply realizing how many details, to-do's, and problems to solve are flying all over your brain, trying to find where they are supposed to go, and then watching and noticing the stress of trying to remember and handle them all. Monkey Mind seems like a distant, emotionally indulgent memory when one is living in Parent Mind. There is simply no time to go bananas, to emote, to chest-thump, to fantasize, or even to react with anything but "gotta get it done" when there is so much to simply manage.

How Do I Start a Meditation Practice?

How do you start meditating, so you can actually begin experiencing this phenomenal relationship with your mind and all of the transformation that ensues? There are volumes of books written on all things meditation, including detailed information on posture, hand position, concentration and insight, from many traditions. If you are brand new to meditation, it would be helpful to read up or find a sitting group to get you started.

It's important to know from the onset that meditation is NOT just sitting quietly while your thoughts run amuck. If you sit on a cushion in a quiet place with a Buddha statue and a tinkling fountain holding mala beads and a rosary and a picture of a guru and spend the entire time imagining the best way to let your husband have it when you get home because you are sure that he let the kids have too much junk food while you were out meditating, then you have not meditated. You have spent thirty precious minutes stewing in the muddy soup of your mind, and maybe making more mud to boot.

The physical practice of meditation comes in three primary forms: sitting meditation, walking meditation, and mindfulness practice. Most traditions emphasize sitting meditation as your primary form, interspersed with periods of walking meditation. A typical Zen practice would be 15-25 minutes of sitting followed by 5-10 minutes of walking, followed by 15-25 minutes of sitting. A Theravada practice would do 20-30 minutes of walking followed by 20-30 minutes of sitting, alternately. You can play with your balance of sitting and walking depending on the amount of time you have to meditate on any given day, your physical needs, and how your concentration is faring.

If you are brand new to meditation, start small. Spend five minutes of sitting and walking alternately and build up your time as it feels right for you. It is best to set an alarm for each session, so that you can fully immerse and don't have to keep checking the clock. Try to pick a nice-sounding alarm; they even have singing bowl ringtones these days, so you don't have to be jolted from your meditative state by the ninja robot sounds your 8-year old son downloaded or tacky pre-programmed digital imitations of classic rock songs.

Then, for the rest of your day, work towards an ever-increasing mindfulness meditation practice. You'll discover quickly that the three practices complement each other well. There are supportive practices too that can only enhance and amplify your meditation experience and benefits, such as yoga, spiritual dancing like zikr, and devotional chanting such as kirtan.

For the sake of getting started properly, here is a primer on all three types of meditation practice:

Sitting Meditation. Find a quiet location. Sit on a pillow, meditation cushion, or chair with an erect posture. Your sitting bones should be comfortably balanced on your left and right sides, equally supporting your torso. Legs should be crossed if on a cushion, or uncrossed and flat-footed if on a chair. Hands can rest on your knees or in your lap.

Begin to notice your breathing. When you inhale, breathe into the belly and relax your shoulders. Say to yourself: "I am breathing in." When you exhale, notice the complete release of air from your belly and chest, and say to yourself: "I am breathing out." As you do this, begin to observe the three possible states of your mind. If you are in Still Mind from the beginning, then fully relax into Still Mind.

If you are in Monkey Mind, then you would work with your thoughts as follows:

"I'm bored! I hate being bored! I'll go crazy this way! 25 minutes on this cushion? Forget it! I want chocolate!" As soon as you catch your mind swirling into these thoughts, tag them THOUGHTS. Refocus on your breathing. Continue to observe as your mind begins again: "Great. Now that it's quiet I am thinking about Cody's teacher. She doesn't like me. I know she doesn't. She talks to all the other parents and smiles and laughs with them, but not with me. I probably intimidate her or something. I probably said something really inappropriate about her hair. I always do that. Why do all the other moms always know just what to say but not me? Did they all take a class or something? Or maybe Cody isn't doing as well as I thought he is. Maybe there's a serious problem. Oh my God, what if Cody is held back three grades?" Again, no matter how far the train of thoughts might have left the station, stop when you notice it chugging along with the intentional force of the tag word THOUGHTS. Return to your breathing. Repeat this process until the alarm goes off.

If you are in Parent Mind, the technique is similar to the one described above, albeit with different thought patterns. To wit:

Breathe in. Notice and say to yourself, "I am breathing in." Breathe out. Notice and say to yourself: "I am breathing out." Repeat until Parent Mind thoughts creep in: "I forgot Cody's permission slip. Dang. I think today's the last day to get it turned in so he can go to the Hard Rock Geology Museum. Where is it? Oh yeah—on my desk under the electric bill. I have to pay that bill by 5pm. Can't forget. Permission slip, electric bill... wait, is today the dentist or is it tomorrow? They texted me yesterday. Better check my phone as soon as I get up... dang I need to know so I can plan the day...." Catch yourself and give this train of thinking the tag word PLANNING. Then return to inhaling and exhaling, labeling every breath in and every breath out. Resist the excruciating temptation to get off the cushion to check your calendar, email, or phone, even if your thoughts do this: "I could sit much more comfortably if I just quickly check my text and know what day that appointment is. And put the permission slip and bill in my purse so I don't forget them. Then I can sit the rest of the time without worrying." DON'T MOVE. Tag those thoughts too, and return to your breathing focus.

Of course, it is entirely likely that your meditation will consist of combinations of these types of mind states, from Still Mind to Monkey Mind to Parent Mind. One small thought can set off a whole chain reaction, and then your mind really starts to party. But you only have one job: focus on your breath, be watchful of any and all thoughts that take you away from your breath, and when you find them, return to your breath. That's it.

Often, people ask: "but what if it's a really important thought? Wouldn't meditation be a great time to work it through? Or what if it's something I need an answer for, or something I want to manifest? Wouldn't putting all my focus on making something happen that I want to happen be a great way to meditate?" There is certainly a time for that, but not during your dedicated sitting practice. One effective strategy, however, is to set an appropriate intention *before* you begin your practice. For example, before you begin, simply state: "I wish for relief for those beings suffering from the tsunami." Or, "I wish for clarity and peace so that I may work through my financial struggles to the benefit of all beings." Then let it go, take a deep beginning breath, and dive into your practice. It is best NOT to set an intention like: "I wish I will get a new job that will make me visible to millions, and all my clothes will be pink and sparkly." Not only is this type of intention not in the spirit of meditation, but the Universe has a great sense of humor: it may just grant you this wish in ways you didn't intend, and you'll find yourself the national poster child for a new glamorous brand of vegetarian wiener, parading around in a pink hot dog costume.

Walking Meditation: In walking meditation, the movement of the body brings a fresh perspective to your practice. Walk slowly and purposefully, allowing each foot to fully experience contact with the floor, grass, or ground. Put all of your focus on the sensation of your feet in relationship to the ground. Allow yourself to feel gratitude for the support. Notice which part of your foot is touching the ground at any given moment. Completely absorb your focus into this sensation. Keep your eyes only half open. If you begin to notice that you haven't clipped or painted your toenails in weeks, lower your lids a bit more and return to the sensation of the contact of your feet with the ground. Begin to coordinate your breathing with your walking; for example, breathe in as the left foot moves, then breathe out as the right foot moves.

This wonderful combination of rhythm, sensation, breathing, and focus often makes walking meditation a bit easier for beginners, since the effort required to focus on several things at once can help reign both Monkey and Parent Minds in if they get off and running. It also creates a nice dynamic with sitting meditation. A word of caution, however: Walking meditation can backfire when it morphs into a walk to the bathroom to touch up your toenail polish, or to the kitchen for a glass of water, or to your desk, or to your phone for a quick check on that nagging dentist appointment. As with sitting meditation, sometimes the most successful meditation is simply staying intently with your practice despite your visceral desire to break away, even for "just a minute." Label this feeling DISTRACTION. Keep walking all the way through your allotted time with your primary foci as home base: your feet, the ground, and your breath. Even if your mind doesn't cease its chatter, congratulate yourself for staying with it all the way through, and know you will have more opportunities to practice with these sensations.

Mindfulness Practice: Unlike the more formal practices of sitting and walking meditation, mindfulness practice is the "meditation in motion" that you endeavor to do for the rest of your day. It is, simply put, your effort to become fully present with every experience in every moment. Whenever you can, remember to just notice what you are doing, hearing, feeling, and sensing, without getting caught up in these things. It is helpful to use the actual sounds, sights, smells, and tastes of the world to help key you to this practice. Every time a sensation is engaged, use it to remind you to take a deep, nourishing breath and, if only for a second, fully embrace that sensation. Here is an example:

You're at the grocery store. You've already gone over your budget, and you haven't finished getting some basic things on your shopping list for the week's meals. Your two year old has a full diaper and smells terrible. Your six year old is begging you for cookies in his whiniest, most caustic voice. You are sleep deprived and irritable. Suddenly, you catch a pungent whiff of your toddler's diaper. Voila! Sensation! The practice here is to simply stop for a moment and step back from the ensuing tumult of the mind, fully smelling the horrible poopy smell, fully hearing the high pitched whining of your older child, fully feeling your exhaustion, fully observing your shallow breathing from the stress and worry over your budget limitations, fully noticing without judgement or further thinking. Put a "pause" button on your mind's habitual tendencies to go on with "oh man, how am I gonna get this diaper changed and get my son to quiet down? Everyone is looking at me. They think I am a horrible mother. I don't even have enough energy to push this cart, never mind deal with the rest, and I don't even have enough money for the peanut butter we need, and..."

STOP. Just for this moment, play with allowing the smell, the sound, and the feeling to exist by themselves. Breathe in and out. Notice some more. Then, be it one second or two minutes later, proceed with the tasks at hand. Try this mindfulness technique whenever you think of it—when your phone rings, when someone honks their horn in a traffic jam, when your son screams "MOOOOOOMMM!" The extra seconds you allow yourself to be mindful will prove to be utterly transformational.

A final bit of advice: when you meditate in any form, do so with absolute authenticity and earnestness. To quote the classic Zen Sandokai, also known as the Identity of Relative and Absolute: "I respectfully say to those who wish to be enlightened: Do not waste your time by night or by day."[v] In other words, to pursue meditation with a lackadaisical intention defeats its purpose. Open your heart wide, sit with sincerity, prepare to meet yourself fully, and experience the unfolding.

Tip #1:
The Four Noble Truths of Parenting and the Path

The Buddha laid out what are called the Four Noble Truths[vi], and they are considered the foundation for all spiritual seekers. Here they are, simplified and modified for moms and dads:

1) With the considerable demands of parenting, there will be times when you really feel suffering. And OY, when you feel it, does the rest of the family feel it, too.

2) The reason we suffer is usually because we have unrealistically high expectations of ourselves as parents, of the world, and of people around us (i.e. we get sick—not supposed to happen! Our child misbehaves—not supposed to happen! I can't finish all my work in time—not supposed to happen! I am not a perfect mom/meditator as I see what perfect is supposed to be— not supposed to happen!). With our constant efforts to mold ourselves and the world around us so these expectations can be met, comes predictable disappointment, fatigue, heartache, etc., aka *suffering*.

3) There is a way to end this cycle of suffering. The whole world benefits from this "Way." You do not have go to any extremes like leaving your family to go on a lifelong pilgrimage to the Himalayas or live as an ascetic in the woods and eat oak leaves for twelve years, nor is the Way to win the lottery and have all worldly needs compensated for (although occasional pedicures are really nice). It is often called "The Middle Way."

4) The Middle Way involves concerted daily focus on right

choices, as defined in the Eightfold Path, and is worth studying. The Middle Way involves getting to know your mind and your extremes, and finding center. For example, parents often oscillate between the edges of exhaustion and mania. Learning through meditation what your tendencies and triggers are will allow you to recognize these tendencies and coax yourself lovingly to a state of balance, and hence end the roller coaster.

Ultimately, it is your very clear intention to end suffering via meditation and the daily action of sending love to yourself and to others that will set you—and those around you—free. Not only your family, but the whole world will find peace at last through this Way, and yes, mom and dad, it all starts with *you*. There is a reason spiritual deities have names like "Holy Father," "Divine Mother," "Mother Earth," "Father Sun," and the like. As parents, we have been endowed with a mighty big mission from the All, one full of miracles, magic, connection, and awareness beyond boundaries or gates. Enjoy, or at least notice and fully experience, every moment.

Tips 2-5:
Getting Started

Tip #2: Allow your kids to honor your meditation time. Tell them that they may play, read, or do homework quietly while you sit, following household safety rules. When you hear something crash and/or explode, mindfully rise from your cushion and stay present with your emotions, noticing them fully before moving forward with the appropriate response.

Tip #3: If your beautiful white meditation shawl from India is smeared with peanut butter, it is perfectly acceptable to use a blanket with Spongebob Squarepants/Disney Princesses on it instead.

Tip #4: Find a quiet place inside. Because that's the only place it's going to be quiet....

Tip #5: We meditate to connect to our Source, aka Allness, Suchness... and as we practice, this connection permeates everyday life. As such, we infinitely do laundry, cooking, and dishes. Simultaneously, there are no dishes, cooking, or laundry. This is a good thing, for those of us who have no maid.

Tips 6-8:
Breathing, Time, and School Camping Trips

Tip #6: In the rapid-fire world of active parenting—you know, when your three-year old is hanging from the top of the bookshelf (inexplicably, as he was just playing with blocks two seconds ago before you turned your head) while you are trying to talk to an important client, the black beans are burning, your baby is crying, your nine-year old is asking you to explain why we aren't doing more about global warming, and your husband is shouting for clean, matching socks—all at the same time—it is easy for the yogic/Zen techniques of "fully experiencing every moment" to unravel. So what to do? Notice you are breathing through all of it. Breathing is nice. Breathing is enough. Noticing it is enough. After all, it means we are alive on this little spinning floating planet to be able to do all of this crazy stuff, and that is nothing short of miraculous.

Tip #7: Invariably, and no matter how you plan it with naptimes, getting up extra early, waiting till your kids are at school, etc., your preschooler will somehow time into the exact moment you have just settled into perfect, blessed, long-awaited stillness on your cushion and need you RIGHT THEN. I once even had a phone call from the preschool reporting that my son was sick and crying for me at the very moment I sat down to meditate. This is not a conspiracy against your meditation practice. It is a cosmic reminder that you have been given a few precious years to be the center of another being's heart, and that in no time at all you will have all the time in the world to meditate... and during those times, you will wish for your kids instead. This is the practice... without linear time, shape, boundaries, or form.... Only This.

Tip #8: It can be very challenging to maintain a meditation practice while on a school camping trip with one hundred over-excited fifth graders, especially when the cabin you are assigned to is full of nine- and ten-year old girls who are afraid of cockroaches, spiders, and the dark, the love bugs and mosquitoes want to very proactively get to know you, the mattresses squeak like someone is slowly and excruciatingly letting the air out of a very large, loud balloon, one of the only two toilets is backed up, and your bunk mate snores in such a forceful and regular way that you are convinced, in half-wakefulness, that we need to evacuate for an impending tornado. Put bug spray on and find a pre-dawn spot with a view of the lake and oak tree sentries all around, enjoying the sounds of the night creatures catching up with the first dawn birds, breathe in this wonderful temporary stillness and nestle it inside, knowing that it, and about six gallons of sweet tea, will sustain the day.

Tips 9-12:
Cartoons, Starting Over, Fairies, and Personal Grooming

Tip #9: Saturday morning can be an excellent time for an extended meditation sit if you are all right with your children watching a few Saturday morning cartoons while they nibble on bagels and fruit. I personally am fine with a couple of educational PBS kids shows, even if my ten-year old would much prefer "My Babysitter's a Vampire" over "Curious George." If you feel guilty about all the TV-watching while you meditate, however, welcome the guilt—it will give you something to work with during your sit.

Tip #10: There are some days that, despite a good run of daily meditation, insights, yoga, healthy eating, exercise, and a comfortable sense of being on your path, that you wake up and just cannot get it together. You can't quite wake up, you are only partially attentive to your kids, the deafening sounds of the high school sports teams waiting in the four-mile long line at Burritos-R-Us (where your kids just HAD to go) is about to drive you insane, your neck is stiff from sleeping funny, and you basically wish you could just start over but it's already 3pm. I call this the "one step forward two steps back" principle. It is insidious because it gives the illusion that your meditation practice isn't working. Don't let this principle deter you. It too is an illusion and an important part of the practice. The key is to start over right then, right there, somewhere between ordering the "Number Three Beany Burrito with Belly Buster Fries and a Drink" and asking your preschooler to wait three more minutes before going to the bathroom, hoping he doesn't do a belly buster right there on the floor. Start noticing your breath. Start noticing your feelings, your physical sensations, your moment as it is at 3pm. Start over.

Tip #11: By all means, permit your kids to meditate with you if they are interested. But they may not need it. When my daughter was four, she asked me why I meditate. I told her it was because it was the only way I could see the Fairies in the Forest. Her reply: "Oh! I get it. So I don't need to meditate, 'cuz they are always playing with me." At 10, she says she still sees them or feels their presence about every day. Still, sometimes both of my kids will come and sit on my lap during meditation time and we will "watch for the Fairies." Nothing more needs to be done at this point, unless your now five-year old son decides to freeze them with his imaginary ice blaster ray gun. Such incidences provide a great opportunity to teach these young grasshoppers about loving kindness and the mindset of "do no harm." Where we live, we have beautiful native vines with yellow flowers that mysteriously appear on the ground even where there are no vines. My son loves them, and we call them "Fairy Flowers." When he learned that ice blasting the fairies would make the flowers disappear, he resolved to just "tranquilize" the fairies instead. I surrendered.

Tip #12: Many parental units say that they barely have any time for basic grooming, like shaving, tweezing, or showering—never mind time for meditation. However, one of the many benefits of meditation is that more of the finer details of life's experiences are noticed and tended to in harmony with the natural flow, since one is not as caught up in the maelstrom of thought and all of its anxious, manipulative tendencies. Hence, it is much more likely that you will notice and tend to your unibrow, nose growths and/or your "eau de musk" in a timely fashion. In other words, when you learn to let go through meditation, it's less likely that your mother-in-law will report to the rest of the family that you've "let yourself go."

Tips 13-16:
Angel Wings, Control, Acceptance, and Martyrdom

Tip #13: Sometimes, after one has established a meditation practice, it is common to experience weight gain, including flabby triceps and glutei. This effect is due to the release of stress, as worry and anxiety burn calories, and the release of tension can slow the metabolism. My friend Roswita calls this the "Angel Wing Effect." It often deters new meditators from continuing with their meditation due to a particular level of totally freaking out that makes them want to spend that precious 30-45 minutes for a second run on the treadmill instead of a single sit on the zafu cushion. If one can breathe through and get past this stage, one may find that they eventually become much healthier inside and out, and confident enough to bare any kinds of arms they wish.

Tip #14: Sometimes, despite the right conditions, proper allotment of time, a quiet space, etc., your "Monkey Mind" will simply not ease off during your entire sit. Sometimes, in fact, it even seems to get more hyper, leaving one with a sense that their meditation for the day has been for naught. This is not at all dissimilar to the indescribably frustrated feeling you have when, despite all of your best efforts, your four-year old simply will not get to sleep, and instead wants to play "Alien Cash Register" on his pillow until midnight with lots of loud BEEP BEEP BEEPing sounds, even though at 5:45pm he was close to drifting off but you redirected him from falling asleep so he wouldn't be awake all night and you were so proud because for SURE he would fall asleep at 8pm, and then you could meditate.... This experience is not a waste of time and energy, nor an example that you are losing control. Rather, it is a great chance to bow to the mysterious force that Einstein credits for all of the indescribable events that remind us that we are NOT the ones in control of our micro-universes, and certainly not the big "Universe" itself, though we sure love to try. It can be met with laughter, albeit occasionally it comes out sounding a bit maniacal.

Tip #15: Up at 5am. Hit snooze; miss morning meditation. Up for real at 5:40. Lunches are made, kids are dressed and fed and off to school, errands are done, phone calls and tests and emails are returned, dog poop is picked up, ninety minutes till time to get kids; FINALLY time to meditate. Right? Wrong. Husband: "The car broke. We have to go and take it in to the mechanic, NOW." Notice feelings: Dejected. Sad. Disappointed. Notice that the feelings are in the stomach. Remember a great quote from a master: "Happiness, according to me, means acceptance of what-is in any situation. The ultimate happiness is contentment, and contentment means acceptance, not 'wanting' happiness. Not seeking happiness means accepting whatever is at the moment. Acceptance means acceptance of happiness or unhappiness, as it happens. Acceptance means surrender and surrender means expecting no change, wanting no change. Everything happens. Nobody does anything."

— *Ramesh Balsekar, THE END OF DUALITY*[vii]

Tip #16: Proactive parents are notorious martyrs. We spend most of the hours in each day, most days of each week, and most weeks of each month making sure our kids are eating vegetables and avoiding trans fats, artificial colors and high fructose corn syrup, getting enough sleep, brushing their hair and teeth, dressing in clothes that are neat or at least clean, making sure they read, learn, and artistically express themselves. All the while, we neglect our own personal nutrition, fitness, appearance, artistic and educational interests. My mother, Deborah Townsend, was keenly aware of this double standard and had a hilarious saying: "Do as I say and not as I do!" And yet, we loved it most when she did take care of herself and pursued her own passions. It is most ironic that the one thing a parent can do that helps everyone in the family—meditation—is often at the bottom rung of the personal parental priority list, somewhere between painting toenails and going salsa dancing. In approximately the time it takes to fold a hamper of bath towels, one can accomplish a decent sit. The household will thank you for it, and it is way better to assign crumpled up towels as martyrs than yourself.

Tips 17-20:
Sitting Space, Hormones, Doer-Ship, and Hunger

Tip #17: It is helpful to have an established sitting space, dedicated just to meditation. My sitting area is a part of the living room with a small table that has a Buddha statue, a picture of St. Francis surrounded by lots of animals, a statuette of the Hindu musical mother goddess Saraswati, mala beads, a mezuzah, and small bamboo arranged upon it, with a zafu sitting cushion within easy reach. The family agrees that there are to be no toys, cheese crackers, etc. anywhere near this small sanctuary, and it usually works.

Tip #18: There are many words for it: PMS, male PMS, testosterone overload, menopause, male menopause, hormone imbalance, elevated pregnancy hormones, elevated male empathy pregnancy hormones, etc. to explain the erratic, over-emotive, and sometimes overwhelming behavior that all human beings display at one time or another. It can feel like these invasive biochemicals are swallowing you whole. But there is part of you NOTICING that you are feeling overwhelmed and over-emotive and at the mercy of this ancient biological force. So the next time you break out into tears because a TV commercial for life insurance shows a child, now grown, kissing his mother goodbye as he goes off to college, with a cheesy bellowing violin and keyboard track intensifying the unbearable experience, just take a moment and ask yourself: who's feeling? Then, by all means, bawl your eyes out, with no reservation or judgment or conservation of tissues. Allowing life to move through you as you feel and express is meditation in action.

Tip #19: On "Doer-ship": If there is food in front of us, we do eating. If there are dirty dishes or laundry in front of us, we do washing. If there is a book in front of us, we do reading. If our children are in front of us, we do parenting. If there is a floor/cushion/chair in front of us, we do meditation. If there is a "To Do" list in front of us, we put meditation at the top of the list.

Tip #20: When you are physically hungry, you may feel unease, and so you eat. The wise, mindful person eats broccoli and chia seeds. The distracted, monkey-minded person eats fries and burgers. When you are spiritually hungry, you may feel unease, and so you seek to feed that hunger. The wise person meditates. The distracted, monkey-minded person watches TV, drinks too much beer, or plays video games. When you are a parent, your children model these choices. So when one believes that they must wait until their kids are grown and off on their own before establishing or returning to a meditation practice, consider what one is representing as wisdom to their children, and what one is really hungry for.

Tips 21-23:
Beginner's Mind, Butts, and Hurricanes

Tip #21: Meditation, like parenting, is an organic—not linear—practice. You don't start as a beginner, go through some sort of formulaic progression of steps that need to be checked off, and end up enlightened or done with parenting. Funny thing is, it usually feels that way for quite some time. You do things by the book, you feel inner peace and a higher connection to a deeper source, and get a sort of spiritual illusion of "wisdom" that comes with being "experienced." You do things by the book, your child grows and appears happy and more independent, and you feel a similar sense of confidence that you are an experienced parent. But when you least expect it, both your practice and your child will need you more than they've ever needed you before, and with an earnestness that reminds us that we are all beginners. That is where real wisdom resides.

Tip #22: Last night, I came home all blissed out after meditation and chanting to get my kids into bed, told them a fabulous story about enlightenment, and the little Buddha darlings started drifting off to sleep. Then, about three minutes later, my son says: "Butt." And then my daughter says "Butt." And then my son says "Butt FACE!" Daughter: "Double gassy butt FACE!!!" "Butt!!" "FACE butt!" "Butt on your FACE!" "BUUUUTTTTT FAAACE WITH POOOOOP!"

"POOOOPY DOUBLE POOP BUTT FACE!!!" I noticed my reaction. My real self wanted to laugh, but the "parent" self knew I should tell them to stop and go to sleep. Conflict. Laugh? Reprimand? Both? Times like these, follow SBRFAD: Stop, Breathe, Relax, Feel, Allow. Then Do. At this moment there was only one thing to do. Me: "Benny Albert and Grace Ohana Smith!!!!!" Them, trying not to crack up: "Yes, mommy?" Me, after a pause: "BUTT!"

Tip #23: Here in Florida, we talk about hurricanes a lot. The other day, my daughter was asking me about the eye of the hurricane. We talked about how it is supposed to be very beautiful and almost mystically calm when the eye passes over. She noted that "If a really big hurricane comes, I would find my way to the eye and just stay in there." My meddling monkey mind thought about this for a moment and chimed in: "Oh, no. The eye is right in the middle of it. You'd be stuck. How would you get out? What if you can't stay there and the worst parts of the hurricane are right there? Best to get as far from the hurricane as possible." My daughter's response: "Momma, you can just stay in the eye until the hurricane eventually runs out of energy. Then you are never blown away, you never panic, and you get to experience something really amazing." Whoa. Never, EVER underestimate the natural Divine wisdom of a ten-year old. See you in the Eye.

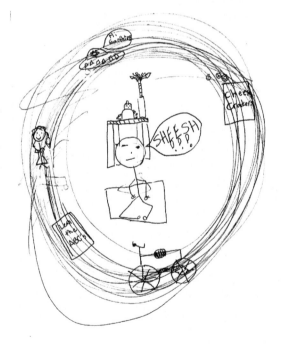

Tips 24-27:
Oneness, Tween Drama, Sleep, and Innocence

Tip #24: Meditation brings us into Oneness. There is no small "I", no bubble of the individual.... Only the big "I" of the ocean, the infinite, connected awareness. But should you ever feel disconnected, look no further than the natural, daily interactions with your own kids or loved ones. Their happiness is your happiness. Their pride in achievements is your own pride and joy. Their grief cuts through your heart deeper than if you were the one having the direct experience. Take any elementary-aged soccer game, when two dads might either slug or hug each other in direct proportion to what their sons are doing out in the field, or any exhausted middle-schooler trying to finish her homework late at night while their parent's hearts' and bodies similarly ache from the fatigue and frustration, or any mom that has sobbed with her five-year old when her beloved pet hamster Fluffy dies. There is no "you" and "them," no mind creating separation. You are in these perfect moments absolutely together, and your Source is the same.

Tip #25: Many of us get into meditation because emotions can be overwhelming at best, and at worst get us into a lot of trouble, whether in our love lives, anger management situations, feelings of self-loathing, or worse. Emotions are often the result of hormones, which affect the brain and give the illusion that feelings are really, really, important. Just ask any tween or teen who dramatically bemoans: "NO ONE UNDERSTANDS ME!!!" Emotions are real. They can suck. They can get us into real trouble well into adulthood if we don't learn how to manage them early on. So how do you explain to your tween that emotions are NOT the all-knowing guideposts of Truth? That they are just another part of experiences that will come and go? If you start "talking spiritual," it will backfire. You will get the classic eye roll and groan and your tween will fall more deeply into a state of morose brooding. Better to give her the real-life example of your high school crush, Steve. Explain to her that Steve was your whole world. Steve walked on water. You lived and breathed Steve, and no one understood how incredible he was except for you. Then your best friend started dating Steve. You couldn't believe the betrayal. For weeks, you stewed in the heartbreak and shame, taking it out on friends and family without mitigation. Then Steve broke your best friend's heart. Steve was a jerk. He was a serious loser. Your best friend cried for weeks, and you realized that it could have been you in that situation. Your emotions were—dare we say it?—WRONG about Steve. You wasted five weeks of your life living and breathing an illusion and dumping your heavy feelings all over your poor friends and family instead of going to the beach and having fun. So you learned to let go. You comforted your friend, and you moved on, and you still have your same best friend to this day.

In meditation, we practice allowing for ALL of these things to happen, because they will, because we are human vessels with emotions and pain. When you share these stories with your adolescent, you teach by example while bathing them in love, understanding, and connection, allowing those difficult experiences to bring us to awareness and move beyond them, opening space for infinite Love and gratitude. Then you can both get back to the business of preparing for her next Big Drama, and await with open arms and a big tissue box.

Tip #26: Sleep is underrated. This whole modern world concept of "pushing through" and "toughing it out" and "sacrificing" as a way of life is bunk. If you are totally sleep deprived as a parent, you are at best barely functional and at worst a safety hazard. If you are sleep deprived when you meditate, you'll probably just pass out. If you are already sleep deprived and you set your alarm extra early to meditate before waking the kids up, fuggetaboutit.

Tip #27: Children have a way of interpreting, utilizing, and expressing the spiritual/yogic/ meditation teachings in their own unique ways. Because we are adults with lots of stories—aka baggage—that can affect or infect our interpretations, these unique expressions of children can irritate us and make us feel we need to correct them towards the "proper" way of expression, or, better yet, bring us back to total innocence if we let them. Take my five-year old son for example, who, like most young children, is full of unique and hilarious expressions. Today, I asked him to use a mindful "Yoga Nidra" type of body scan to help him get to sleep for naptime. So he did, a la: "Go to sleep, eyes! BAM!!!" (hitting his face close to his eyes). "OW! HAHAHAHHA! Go to sleep, head! SUPER ZOP!!!!" (punching self on the head), "OWWW! HAHAHAHHAHA! Get yourself to sleep, ears! WHAAMMMMOO!" (boxing himself on the ears), "YOUCH! BWAAAAAA HAAHAHA!" Unbelievably, he passed out in three minutes.

Tips 28-30:
Cacophony, Freedom, and Being Sick

Tip #28: A great time to really "hear" all the thoughts in your mind and work with them is in the deep quiet of the very early morning, free of the hum of all the family and household noises, and ideally when meditating. But sometimes, when you have to leave extra early for work and you try really, really hard not to wake up the rest of the family (who seem to know when you are trying not to wake them up and you know they are surely going to wake up any minute now), listen to the cacophony of your thoughts. If the sheer volume, variety, and intensity of your thoughts concern or upset you, then you are still caught in your mind. Notice that, and let that be your perfect practice at that moment. If, on the other hand, you find the whole experience to be hilarious, or, as "The Untethered Soul" author Michael Singer[viii] endearingly says in his dharma talks: "cute and adorable," then you are in your soul's seat and can start your day with some ecstatic giggling.

Tip #29: In meditation, the teachings as expressed through dharma talks, readings, koan studies, and the like are often described as "beacons" or "pointers" toward enlightenment, or lifeboats to help take you Home. On the path, they can frustrate the practitioner, because the rational mind can't quite wrap around the words. And yet, if we can keep from thinking too hard or getting frustrated, we are somehow naturally driven to keep going after them and are gifted breakthroughs along the way. Afterwards, we respectfully part ways with each beacon after it has done its job.

Your child's natural evolution is a good model for this process. Take potty training and reading as examples. In the former case, we try and try for our toddler to become free of diapers by buying him a Prince Elmo potty trainer that plays "You Are My Sunshine" with lights that twinkle when Elmo's voice sings: "You did it!" And yet, your child continues to use his diaper, despite his apparent delight and curiosity at Prince Elmo's pomp and bling. Day after day, devotedly, you practice with him. And then, one day, he is no longer in diapers. Prince Elmo, once the center of your universe, goes to the thrift store donation bin.

In the latter case, your child sees letters and words and pictures and it all looks like a bunch of gobbledygook for years, and yet she is driven to keep staring at them, processing them somehow, and then one day, she reads.

There is not much difference between these examples and the deciphering of mystical sayings and koans, save for one big difference: with our practice, our big fat mind likes to get in the way. Look to your child, beautiful and surrendered to his/her natural, innate abilities and patient perseverance to become free, without self-imposed obstacles.

Tip #30: Sometimes you catch a really nasty bugger of a cold from your son who caught it last week from some coughing, stuffed-up kid he was playing with in school. If you're really rocking, your daughter catches it too and she gets uncharacteristically cranky and whiney, which, since you are sick too, is enough to drive you bananas. To top it all off, just as the worst of the cold is barraging you with its whole gloppy, merciless effect, your son-who-started-it-all is almost completely better and only wants to be as wild as he can possibly be to make up for all the other days he was lying around. A sit-down meditation is totally out of the question, since your nose alone won't allow you to sit for more than two seconds without requiring a tissue, and your son is trying to climb up on your shoulders at the same time, and your head is so congested and swirly that you can't even make sense of your thoughts, no less watch them or let them go. You go into major "do something about it" mode: pull out the echinacea, vitamin C, neti pot, garlic, manuka honey, neem, ginger, astragalus, loquat syrup, green tea, and legal or maybe illegal drugs, and try to trudge through the day in misery with some nice kvetching at your husband thrown in for maximum effect, while you dutifully go through the motions of cleaning and cooking and laundry and social networking and bugging your kids to clean up their messes and practice piano. Can you let that all go? There is only one thing to do here: Be sick.

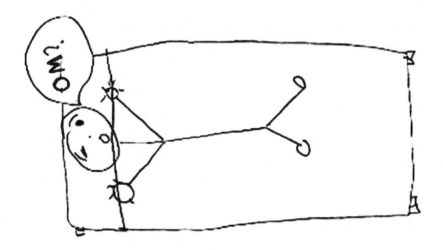

Tips 31-33:
Word Doohickeys, Kindergarten Wisdom, and Mother Bear

Tip #31: Just cleared my fridge of about a million of those little "Magnetic Poetry for Kids" doohickeys. They were wonderful when we first got them—we made all kinds of creative, brilliant, and witty sentences—but that was a few weeks ago and now they have disintegrated into a bunch of word debris infecting every corner of my fridge.

While mindfully removing piece after piece, I visualized simultaneously removing thought debris from my brain. Just like the doohickeys, our brain has an amazing capability of creating brilliance from small parts. But then it just keeps them all in there like a good little data processor until they unravel and float about, further obscuring our efforts for potential cleanliness of our mind. In the Buddha's teaching, "the criterion of genuine enlightenment lies precisely in purity of mind."[ix] Are there any similar, metaphorical models for your mind in your physical world that you can purify?

Tip #32: When I asked my five-year old son why mommy meditates, he said: "Because it makes you feel good. And it gives you castle kingdoms. And you say thanks for the castles and kingdoms. And then I stare at Mommy and then she remembers she has things to do like let out the dogs and make my bagel and she stops meditating. But she does it because it's better for her and it helps me because it gives me good dreams because I feel better." There it is: direct evidence, from the mouth of a kindergartener, of one's practice being the practice of all beings.

Tip #33: Most moms, dads, pet parents, and other caregivers have had at least a taste of the power of "Mother Bear": If their child is threatened in any way, all fear or conventional thought disappears and you attain almost super-powers to defend and protect your loved one. I once dove, literally without a thought, into the middle of a violent attack on my dog, grabbed the jaws of a Cujo-sized million-pound Rottweiler and pried him off of my little Schipperke. The sheer laser focus of my mission sent the ginormous canine whimpering away by some unspoken force that came out of me that apparently was something to be reckoned with. I was totally in the moment, without thought or distraction or fear, and was gifted a brief but powerful glimpse of the power of the freedom that this pure state of mind bequeaths. Imagine what we would be capable of if one could maintain this state of mind during the daily, "Nothing Special"[x] routines of life. Without the drama, without the threat but just with the experience the powerful peace of human existence in each moment without suffering.

Tips 34-36:
Slowing Down, Smartphones, and Housework

Tip #34: One phenomenon of this practice is that as you learn to stop fighting with and start surrendering to the reality of your present experience, reality starts dancing the cha-cha with you. To use illness as an example: When I stopped trying to plow through my sickness grudgingly and just relaxed (as much as one can with a head cold) into "being sick," an amazing thing happened. Life slowed waaaaay down. The laundry list was the same: the laundry pile was bigger, the kids' needs were the same, the house was just as messy, the emails were just as extensive, and the daily schedule was just as busy. But somehow everything got slower, and I could hear and see much more beyond the senses that congestion was obscuring. Went to water the garden and discovered that the garden wasn't a place to water and pull weeds from—it just made me happy, and I noticed for the first time that some of the weeds were attracting butterflies. Went to the organic market and consumed massive quantities of locally grown vegetables, and the whole experience of having such a place so close to home and being able to self-nourish so easily summoned swells of gratitude. Languished in a loooong, sinus-opening forward bend. Picked up the kids and just felt like kissing them. Who would've thought that a state of recovery could actually procure a state of Grace?

Tip #35: Got a smartphone? You know, that little palm-sized doodad with all of your emails, Facebook, apps, alarms, calendar appointments, and games? Congratulations, you've got distraction. Got kids? You know, the little hip-high beings who want to throw the damn thing out the window because you are only halfway paying attention to them when the palm-sized doodad is within arm's reach? Congratulations, you've got real live Keepers of the Present Moment.

Tip #36: In "Autobiography of a Yogi,"[xi] after Paramahansa Yogananda attains supreme enlightenment, transcendentally flying through the air and seeing and knowing all, his master greets him on his return with a broom and a smile and asks him to sweep the ashram floor. In Zen, this is called "Chop Wood, Carry Water." When tackling a critical Zen koan called "Joshu's Dog,"[xii] my Zen teacher told me that in order to crack the koan I needed to breathe the ancient Chinese word "Mu," in and out, while washing dishes and doing the laundry. Meditation retreats usually have chores written into the daily practice schedule. So if you think you can't be on this path because you have too many chores to do, guess again—even the great enlightened masters and their students couldn't be absolved from household duties. In fact, household duties are sort of the point.

Tips 37-39:
Surrender, Self-Love, and Sippy Cup Meditation

Tip #37: It is very good to catch your son's cold. It is especially good for it to turn into a very bad case of bronchitis and send you to the doctor for antibiotics. Why? Because people like me rebel against the knock-down, especially after I am convinced that by being on this path I can use all kinds of positive healing affirmations and visualizations of healing light and natural remedies from the garden and breathing and yoga and not need "evil antibiotics." Because I know that this sickness and the immediate need for antibiotics indicates a much greater, life-oriented need to turn inward and really pay attention to a more long-term healing that beckons for a less "go go go" attitude and lifestyle, that allows for imperfection, softness, slowness. That being manically proactive for natural remedies was just another form of "go go go" with a holistic label. To finally go to the doctor was to totally surrender to what I would have once perceived as defeat. It was humbling. It was liberating. Maybe that is what finally elicited the healing, more than the antibiotics.

Tip #38: While there are many multi-faceted and much-numbered principles in Buddhism and other spiritual practices that incorporate meditation, the Dalai Lama bases his teachings on two foundational principles: 1) the interdependent nature of reality, and 2) do no harm/non-violence.[xiii] That means, as a parent, while you would never harm your child, you must never beat yourself up (literally or figuratively) either.

Tip #39: While you may have created a lovely sitting area with Japanese zafu/zabuton sitting cushions and a small shrine with a Buddha and a bamboo on it (and maybe some little crystals with a mala bead necklace going around the whole thing), you may never get there some mornings—like when your small child calls out for you to bring him a yogurt drink in a sippy cup and just lie down with him for a while. These shrine-and-cushion-free mornings do not sacrifice your meditation time. Lying there in the warm, womb-like darkness of pre-dawn is a perfect time to "sit," whether by counting your breaths, counting his sippy cup slurps, working on a Zen koan, or simply doing what's known in Zen meditation as shikan-taza, or "just sitting (lying/walking/jumping/yelling/freaking/fretting/blissing out/etc.)" and noticing all happenings within and without in this very moment.

Tips 40-42:
Lists, We're All Parents, and Cosmic Energy

Tip #40: When one begins a meditation practice, usually the first thing that happens is that one becomes aware of the unbelievable number of "monkey mind" thoughts that are taking over the mind. For mothers, these are usually in the form of "to do" lists: "make lunches, call the pediatrician, buy organic strawberries from co-op, work out, email about PTA meeting, change car tires, fix the tractor, berate self, get solar reactor blueprints to boss by 5pm, fix sewing machine, hem pants, berate self again for not getting enough done in time, help with your daughter's homework, berate self for doing self-berating, find a better swimming coach, don't freak out, freak out, watch self from a higher consciousness freaking out, berate self for freaking out, get mad at husband for not understanding why I am freaking out," etc. As one gets further into the practice, one realizes that there is only one thing for the to-do list: meditate. The rest seems to take care of itself.

Tip #41: We are all the Divine Mother and Father. Even if you don't have physical children—i.e. short growing beings (four-leggeds included) living with you for an extended period of time—your life and work are, as Zen Roshi Valerie Forstman so beautifully describes—your "beloved children." Embrace each element of your life with the fire of love and the song that one sings for the Beloved.

Tip #42: The "meditative state" is described as being reached when one sits through the watching of thoughts and noticing of sensations until, ultimately, thoughts and sensations are minimized (in their impact, though not always in their quantities) and one is in stillness and fully in the present moment. It is in this state that one can receive the very powerful sustenance of "cosmic energy." Not all sits lead to the meditative state, and being in witness is enough. But some sits do reach that state, and the impact of cosmic energy is noticeable. Parenting can be like that, too—most of the time, while you are playing with your child and being a good parent, you are also planning dinner, thinking about work, and organizing the many details of life in your head. But sometimes, your brain takes a back seat and you are actually, fully, PLAYING with your kid and having the time of your life acting like a Power Ranger or kicking a ball. Embrace yourself at those times. Then open your chakras and let the cosmic energy flow in, baby. It may not happen all the time, but when it does, that cosmic energy is some powerful stuff. You need not be sitting on a cushion to receive it.

Tips 43-45:
Busy-ness, Baby Carrots, and Peace

Tip #43: When my kids were born, my mom told me that I was entering "the busy stage of life." And wow, was she right. And wow, do we parents love to talk with each other about the busy-ness of it all. But, as we continue our meditation practice to create space in our experience of life, so too can there be space in the busy-ness. The amount of things that need to be tended to might not change, but our whole approach to it can change drastically, starting with an acknowledgement that our attachment to the busy-ness might be causing suffering. How? By thinking about the state of busy-ness all the time. My guru (mom) always gave this bit of advice: "Saunter." Commiserate less, experience more. Off now to saunter to my desk, then to two meetings, then chores, then car repair (again), then picking up kids, then piano practice, then redirecting my son's new obsession with the word "poop," then dealing with fatigue and runny noses, then homework, then cooking... then counting some stars and breathing in some cinnamon tea. One glorious busy-but-not-busy moment at a time.

Tip #44: Parenting can put you in a constant state of urgency, usually due to the fast pace of taking care of so many little things all day long. When you are beginning to panic because you forgot to cut the organic carrots in cute little circles instead of the long, skinny way, which is how your son used to like it but now he likes the circles, it is time to make some time for meditation. Meditation can really help everything get put into a healthy perspective. At the very least, you begin to watch how silly your mind sounds worrying as much about the shape of your kid's baby carrots as it does on world issues, running away from an attack lion, and saving the planet.

Tip #45: At a recent dharma talk, "The Untethered Soul" author/spiritual teacher Michael Singer spoke of the spiritual path as leading to what Christ called, "The peace that passeth all understanding." This passething thing I totally get. It is understandable that it is hard to feel peace when your three year old is throwing a tantrum about being offered a chia carob bar and not a Kit Kat while forty-two people at the health food store are watching and going "tsk-tsk." It is understandable that you feel at a loss to explain to your devastated tween daughter why orangutans might be extinct in ten years no thanks to human logging and greed. But once you have had a glimpse of the deep stillness beneath the storm of everyday life, you begin to realize with awe that eventually, even catastrophe will not ruffle you. You parent. You give. You receive. You experience. You breathe. You love. You feel. You cry. You laugh. They give. They receive. They experience. They breathe. They love. They feel. They cry. They laugh. It is beyond superficial, mind-based understanding, but who cares? There's nothing at all to figure out, because for some reason, when you reach this state, your son begins to like cruelty-and-chemical-free chocolate, and the orangutans have a real chance because your daughter launches an international pro-habitat, anti-deforestation movement, and the tears flowing from your children's eyes are from their open loving hearts playing their orchestra instead of from frustration and internal cacophony. Like all of nature, giving and receiving are in perfect harmony, as are crying and laughing, sleeping and wakefulness, in balance and in peace.

Tips 46-48:
The Borg, Halloween, and the Oak Tree

Tip #46: Remember the Borg? Those big, bad mammajammas in Star Trek that would find you, no matter where you were in the four quadrants of intergalactic space, and declare ominously: "You will be assimilated. Resistance is futile." Of course, Picard and the Next Generation crew fought valiantly for their individual identities, as would any of us under such circumstances. But the spiritual path is not the same. It's more like there is a presence calling: "I am here, waiting for you at Home, with a depth of peace, love, and understanding that is beyond a single, individual mind's comprehension, and that is your birthright. Whenever you wish to stop resisting, you'll get here." And yet, so many of us still fight this call in the name of this concept of "individuality" or "self-identity" as if that gentle beckoning were from a Borg cubed spaceship, terrified that we will be overtaken if we "let go." Ironically, when one lets go to the fictional Borg in Star Trek, one gets outfitted in a heavy robotic suit and can barely walk. When one lets go to the true reality of the Universe, one soars weightlessly, without burdens. Live long and prosper.

Tip #47: When one becomes a parent, one begins an adventure of awareness that is keenly connected to one or more other deeply feeling beings. It's not "all about you" anymore. The choices you make for yourself, like embarking on a meditation practice, making earth-friendly choices, showing loving kindness to yourself and others, and more, become that much more important to the open-hearted beings you steward. This living, loving practice includes how much Halloween candy you choose to gorge yourself on. At least, show some discretion as to which brands of candy you totally pig out on. Throw in some great memories from your childhood with a few wise words about enjoying the experience without guilt between gooey, chewy, blissfully chocolatey mouthfuls. Do this purposefully and without reservation, even though for the rest of the year one piece of candy alone would drive you into a "teaching moment" about how refined sugar and cheap chocolate causes rotting teeth and pimples and is destroying the planet and promoting unfair trade practices. The next morning, practice mindful quiet sneak-walking when removing a scrumptious York Peppermint Patty from your kids' Halloween basket, and appreciate every secret bite as you eat it for breakfast, throwing in a few childlike giggles between chews.

TIP #48: The next time you are terrifically stressed out because you are late for the orthodontist or unable to get to soccer on time because you can't find your daughter any clean socks or (insert everyday stressor here). Stop for a moment, breathe deeply, and consider the oak tree outside, the air it exchanges life-giving gases with, the clouds that will sooner or later congregate to feed it water. It is unconcerned with dirty socks and missed appointments, but it does face scorching sun, torrential rain, and winds, among other natural stressors. And yet it grows, indescribably beautiful, calm, and upward, and will continue to do so even thirty years from now, when you are worried about being late for your geriatric checkup.

I recently enjoyed a powerful writing by Dennis Merritt Jones[xiv] called "Strong Winds, Strong Roots." He shared that a biodome experiment in the desert demonstrated that trees grown under "ideal" growing conditions of care, water, and sunlight toppled over after they reached a certain height because they weren't exposed to any wind, which was necessary to help the trees develop root structures. Writes Mr. Jones: "We strive to avoid the times of contrast and tension, when life's daily challenges push against us. When they do, the normal tendency is to curse them. If trees could talk, would we hear them curse the wind every time they encountered a storm? Watch how a tree bends and sways gracefully when the wind blows against it. It does not stand rigid, resisting the flow of energy. It does not push back. The tree accepts the strong wind as a blessing that helps it grow." Your meditation practice, like the tree's grace, allows your spiritual roots to grow and ground you while you connect to the sky.

Tips 49-51:
Sssits, Mindful Chewing, and Impatience

Tip #49: Somewhere between a formal, scheduled, and timed sit in a dedicated space and the moment-to-moment mindfulness practice of daily life, there is sometimes the opportunity for what I like to call a "Spontaneous Supervisory Sit," or SSSIT. This opportunity takes place during one of those magical moments when your child or children are playing in a safe setting over an extended period of time, and your only job is to be with them and supervise. You can sit on a bench or cross-legged on a makeshift towel and mind your children and your mind with total presence. Just remember to keep your eyes open.

Tip #50: As I stood in front of the kitchen sink wolfing down handfuls of spinach tortellini because between feeding the family and the animals and cleaning up and helping the kids with homework and picking up not-yet-housetrained puppy poop there was never any time to actually sit down and have a meal for myself, I realized that I was not eating mindfully. I attempted to slow down each chew and carefully experience the sensation of while leaning over the dish-filled sink. By the third chomp, with the dryer buzzing and the TV suddenly turned up with the theme song to Scooby Doo at maximum volume in the background, olive oil dribbling down my chin in a desperate attempt to nourish and work hard at being mindful, and son shouting "Mooooommm!" — I became distinctly aware that the whole scene was hilarious. It was belly-bustingly, life-livingly funny, and the laughter that ensued was a cathartic testament that THIS, ultimately, sums this practice up in one messy, loud, olive-oil basted, Scooby-Doo sound-tracked moment.

Tip #51: One of the interesting things to be attentive to in meditation, parenting, and life in general is impatience. In meditation, you often see impatience in two forms: impatience within the practice itself (intra-impatience), and impatience about the practice (inter-impatience). An example of the former type is when you are immersed in your sit but frustrated with its progress, i.e.: "When will my mind shut up? It's been almost an hour and I want to get beyond this, but I am almost out of time! I need to count my breaths... no, that's not working... what can I do? It wasn't like this yesterday; this shouldn't be happening!" An example of the latter type is when you are on the cushion for all of five minutes but both your mind and body want to be done already and off to the day's doings, and your whole practice is spent using all of your focus and concentration to not get up until your established sitting time is over.

In parenting, we have the same two forms. An example of the former type—intra-impatience—is when you just want your child to move faster, either physically, emotionally, academically, etc., rather than settling into wherever he/she happens to be for however long he/she needs to be there. I.e.: "Why isn't she remembering how to do long division? Yesterday we were doing long division with decimals! Now it's like we never did it! This is driving me crazy! She needs to be ready for algebra if she wants to get into a good college prep high school!" Or:" How long is it going to take him to walk one block? I just want to get there! Why won't he move a little faster? Yesterday I couldn't get him to slow down!" This state of intra-impatience is usually proportional to a parent's state of personal stress, which can compound itself brilliantly with the parent wishing they had time to meditate to alleviate that stress.

The above scenario leads us perfectly to an example of the second type—inter-impatience—which happens when you are there with your child physically but really want to be doing something else, like working on your poetry, working out, cleaning the house without disruption, meditating, and such, and it takes all of your focus and concentration to simply try to stay present with being with the needs of your child.

For both cases of impatience, and in all applications, the approach is the same. Just notice that you have it, give love to yourself and your impatient state, and gently be with it. It will take, er, patience, but it will pass much more quickly than if you go the "instant gratification" route and act on it by jumping off the cushion too soon or giving in to your uptight impulses with your child, rather than simply watching, noticing, and feeling those impulses, even as unpleasant or frustrating as those feelings may be. Eventually, it will go away when you don't hold on to it. And then it will come back. And then it will go away. You'll find that impatience is simply another manifestation of impermanence. And you won't be stuck in any of it.

Tips 52-54:
Grace of Nature,
Saying No and Yes, and Star Wars

Tip #52: Outside in the forest, and deep in the ocean, is a daily battle of life and death, competition for food and light, exposure to sun, wind, storms, currents, hurricanes, and more. And yet, we seek the forest and the sea for their deep tranquility. We leave our burdened lives to find refuge in these places, even if for us lucky folks, our burdens do not include struggles for life, death, food, light, or natural disasters. Our struggles are simply for balance and clarity, financial freedom, a fulfilling job, a great family, a great love life, happiness, a more peaceful and sustainable world, etc.

So why, in the light of our relative struggles, are the deep wild places our source of refuge and seeking? Because the trees, no matter their circumstances, surrender and give their whole existence to the Universe. The fan corals, waving in the currents, are completely at ease with the water's flow. Giving and receiving are in perfect balance. We go to them because they are enlightenment embodied, in harmony, with no mind to get in the way.

Tip #53: Say no. Don't do a lot of extra stuff, or fall into doer-ship without clarity of purpose and space. The more I take off my life's plate, the more I reunite with and appreciate the actual design on the plate itself, which I haven't seen for a good while. But seeing one's actual "plate" is terrifying for a lot of folks. It is so much easier to stuff your plate and avoid looking at your perfect design. And the process of removing "stuff" isn't easy. Hence, you've got a few steps to take: remove the stuff by saying no to distractions, meditate, and stare squarely at the actual plate while feeling everything that comes up when you reunite with your plate's design, aka your true being. You'll find that you might start remembering what it felt like to be a kid, plate open and ready to receive the world, recalling all sorts of childhood stories and relating them to your own children. They'll love it.

That being said, mindfulness will also make you more aware of when saying "yes" will actually create more space on your plate. I'll use a recent example of the dentist. For months, I'd been rescheduling the dentist for our family because it was such a time-consuming ordeal that was compounded by insurance travails, and I was under the illusion that putting it off (and brushing really well) would buy us more time to get on top of all the other "stuff" to create space to finally immerse in the dentist "stuff." No surprise... all of us got toothaches and the dentist stuff compounded into a much bigger time-and-space-taker than if I had just mindfully taken care of the necessity of dental care and maintenance when it first arose.

TIP #54: Want your kids to begin to understand the concepts of prana, aka chi, aka life force, aka shakti, and the importance of focus, concentration, and intention? Watch "The Empire Strikes Back" with particular emphasis on Luke Skywalker's training with Yoda. Let your child become obsessed with light sabers and Storm Troopers or whatever it takes to "hook" them—and discuss Yoda's teachings frequently. I remember, at the age of eleven, only wanting to be one with the Force. Not much has changed. Yoda was my first Buddha.

Tips 55-56:
Tantrums of the Ego
and Personal Growth

TIP #55: At a recent talk at the Temple of the Universe[xv], Mickey Singer likened the tantrums of a young child not getting what he/she wants to the tantrums of the ego when not being fed what it wishes. His teachings, and those of meditation, instruct seekers to simply relax and compassionately let the ego's tantrum pass and not get all tangled up in it, just as you probably would with your child. But we parents get a double whammy when our child has a tantrum in a public place, because often the judgmental or concerned stares of others raises the hackles of your own ego: "This isn't happening to me! They must think I am a horrible parent!" This example is exactly why parenting is an intensive and awesome spiritual practice. It is one of the few life experiences that requires "multitasking" even in your meditation approach, but if you are willing, you can accomplish great feats of awakening by simply viewing these moments, in all of their discomfort, as huge opportunities for letting go, opening, compassion, self-love, outwardly expressed love, and awareness.

Tip #56: When you get sick, even the most experienced meditators can feel challenged in their ability to be present and peaceful with what "is." Meditation teaches us to "unstick" ourselves from the whirlwind of life, to be present to all that is happening without becoming lost in it. But when parents become sick, it's easy to feel as if our whole world is unraveling, since so many others are directly dependent on our well-being. How does one maintain a meditation practice and find center during these times? Practice the ancient art of patience and letting go of your habit of and need to be a constant caregiver. Patience in that despite the fact that you feel like poop while doing the things that MUST be done, like changing the diapers and feeding your kids, you will eventually feel better. Letting go in that maybe, just maybe, your kids will be okay for a day or five if they have a little more movies or frozen dinners than you would allow in your normal state.

And, your kids might just surprise you and benefit from being loosened up a bit from your control. When I was sick recently, my ten-year old learned how to chop vegetables and cook on a hot stove and load and run the dishwasher quite on her own. I supervised wanly, but that was about the extent of my involvement. With my safety paranoia, had it not been for illness, the poor girl might have had to wait until she was sixteen before I allowed her that kind of important personal and creative growth.

Tips 57-59:
Perspective, the Quiet Game, and Family Gatherings

Tip #57: Meditation and many other spiritual practices place much emphasis on the present moment. But in parenting, it sometimes serves to visit the past and future in order to gain perspective on, and fully embrace, the present. Take my five-year old today. We homeschool, so are pretty much in each other's company 24/7. Most of the time, we get into a groove and it's just wonderful. But today, he was overtired and acting very toddler-ish, and I was saturated and about at my wit's end. I gave both of us time outs, during which time I quickly remembered that these "toddler moments" were a regular thing not so long ago, that I didn't even have the luxury of getting tasks done quickly, that I didn't have time to myself, that I couldn't even take a bath like I enjoy regularly now, and that by next year he will be so much more grown that what seems like an infernal eternity right now will soon be a memory, never again to be experienced between us. By the time our mutual time outs were over, the present moment never seemed sweeter.

Tip #58: Modern day parents are given the advice that to boost your child's brain power, phonetic awareness, communication skills, early comprehension abilities, and reading preparedness you should start talking to your child constantly pretty much from birth. Trying to be the best mom ever, I took this advice to heart and began a narrative of every moment with both of my babies, beginning prenatally. Sure enough, and just as the experts portrayed, both of my kids have excellent comprehension and communication skills. In fact, none of us ever shut up. We have become a house of yakkity-yaks, saying things like "bumpity bump" when we drive over a bump, expressing every experience, thought, idea, and emotion in painful detail.

Families are noisy. Kids are noisy. Yet, often we have silent periods; too-long car rides, quiet mornings just waking up or late nights winding down. By habit, we try to fill the silence, but a meditation practice in itself is to resist that temptation, thereby setting the stage for a healthy relationship with silence and the foundation of meditation practice. According to Zen teacher and UU Minister Meredith Garmon: "Out of the silence that words cannot touch comes love—an embracing love of all that is. In spiritual practice, we visit that silence and slowly begin to make a home for ourselves there. Grounded in that home, words are . . . off center. We hear them, we speak them, but they are always a little off to the side—as our eyes rest on the center: on a quiet, shining flame."[xvi]

In 20/20 hindsight, I realize that if I could do it over again, I would devote equal amounts of time to the miracle and magic of silence. We now allow ourselves, and with a good bit of effort, to just be quiet. We actively resist the temptation to say anything. We started by calling it the Quiet Game, but now, with just a few glimpses of the peace and Universe connection, without the distraction of narrative, my kids and I are starting to go there on our own, without giving it a label like Quiet Game or Meditation Time. The experts love to talk about the importance of communication, but through silence we have discovered a communication with Truth that is much, much deeper and more profound, that supersedes developmental benchmarks, time, space, and cool-sounding pseudo-psychological labels.

Tip #59: It is relatively easy to be "spiritual" around friends and acquaintances during short interactions. It is relatively easy to apply the practices of noticing your emotions, judgments, and thoughts. As you relate to them, remain in a centered space, and then go home to your established space to meditate and let go further as needed. Do yoga, or just take a nap if your family is somewhere else and you are in a rare, little-known moment of actually having time to yourself.

It is entirely another thing to be "spiritual" or maintain any kind of practice at all during extended family gatherings in another city when you are sharing a room with all of your kids, next door to "Uncle Snoring Smoking Sol's" room on one side and "Cousin Leroy the Loud Late Night Rated R Movie Watcher" on the other, when the grandparents require frequent bouts of "Quiet Time" at precisely the times when the kids usually have their soccer practice, and your mother-in-law is introducing you to the wonders and conveniences of instant sweet potatoes-in-a-box.

Allow yourself to be soaked in every last "unspiritual" bit of it, along with your inability to escape—think of those who have no families to revel in—and allow this experience to let you notice your judgments and preferences and attachments and work with your relationship to them. Your practice will, contrary to first appearances, evolve exponentially.

Tips 60-62:
Wrinkles, Being-Doing, and Roller Coasters

Tip #60: My late father's face was deeply etched with lines and they were, for the most part, the happiest lines you've ever seen: upturned smiling crow's feet, expressively aware forehead lines, and carefree dimples. There was one clear furrow between his eyes, though, revealing that serious part—the concentration and focus of a scientist, the deep thinking, and the internal demons. For the first time, I am seeing the same pattern of lines beginning to imprint permanently on my own face. And just like his, I adore the happy lines but would gladly Botox the invasive brow furrow away, for it is the one stinker that indicates that I have had more than a few moments in a less-than-la-la state of being.

During meditation, one often experiences great releases in the face: the jaw, the forehead, the eyebrows, the temples. I have watched more than a few parents in deep relationship with their children, with faces squinched up in concentration, frustration, or debilitation, and have started to become mindful of my own. The amount of tension stored in the face is mind-boggling. It even squeezes up like a raisin when I am wrapped up in a yoga pose meant to release something else like the hips or upper back. To be mindful of the face is cathartic, not because it might stave off those pesky wrinkles—"face" it; they're here to stay!— but to achieve a deeper sense of awareness and relation with yourself in the present moment. It has become an integral part of my meditation, not only on the mat but now, especially, during the day-to-day mundaneness, joys, and challenges of parenting.

Tip #61: As beings of the Universe having a human worldly experience, we are able to simultaneously be the experiencers doing the experience and the witnesses to our doer-ship and experience. In meditation, one learns that while the conscious witnessing of the experiences of our life is a constant practice, "doer-ship" need not be constant, and the subtle dance of when and when not "to do" becomes a learned and valuable skill that flows from your being, rather than feeling like your being (as in being happy, being stable, being caught up, being peaceful, being fulfilled) is dependent on what you DO. Over time, you are less and less overwhelmed by the illusion of being drowned in "doing" as a means to get you somewhere "better than here."

According to Dr. David Wolf, author of "Relationships That Work: The Power of Conscious Living"[xvii] and founder of the Satvatove Institute[xviii], we are human beings, not human doings. Says Dr. Wolf: "In the Do-Be paradigm, I am in a mindset that believes 'In order to experience the qualities of my being, I need to do such and such.' That is different than *Be-Do*, where I am living from the consciousness of 'I am complete and whole; I am inspired to do these activities, which naturally intensify and augment my experience of *being*.'"

This skill is very helpful in parenting, an experience which often gives the impression that one must be in a constant state of endless chores, putting out metaphorical fires, and "doing stuff." Dr. Wolf, a father of two, shared with me his personal wisdom about parenting via the Be-Do paradigm as follows: "I see it as important to realize that, while being and doing are different and separate, they're also intimately related. Actually, they're simultaneously distinct and non-different from each other. A healthy consciousness for parents to cultivate is 'An intrinsic aspect of my being is to be the parent of this child. It's no accident that I'm the parent of this particular child.' Parenting starts with 'being.' Being a parent. And, the nature of being is to be active. In connection with parenting, clearly, 'being a parent' certainly includes action." Thus, with just a subtle internal shift of your attention to BEING a parent, and while outwardly looking like you are very busy to others, inwardly each moment is being commanded only by the moment and its full-bodied experience, and in all of its do-ing glory.

Tip #62: I am regularly boggled by and full of gratitude over the miracle and power of intention and surrender. Parents sometimes feel below-par with heavy schedules, heavy constitutions, and heavy neediness from their children. A common usual response is to do more—more for the kids, more supplements, more water, more internet research (maybe we are gluten intolerant? Allergies? More yoga? More meditation? More sleep? Ashwaghanda perhaps? Acupuncture? What to do, what to do?) It gets worse, until you finally just say "I feel crappy. I am offering this crappy feeling to the Universe and asking with faith and love to please help me accept this feeling, to provide me with whatever healing I need because I sure can't seem to figure it out." Then relax into crappiness and wait. Maybe crappiness and heaviness are exactly perfect right now. You won't have to wait too long, because eventually the heaviness will lift and you'll feel great, that is, until the next time you feel crappy, and then great, and then somewhere in-between. Cultivating your deeper place of experience and being allows for a universal acceptance of this heavy-to-light-and-back-again ride, and there is nothing lighter than that. Think of going on the Falcon's Fury roller coaster with your kids. You go up, down, fast, slow, get nauseous, and feel exhilarated all in five glorious minutes. Do you really internalize and agonize over each sensation, or do you just experience it, with FUN as your intrinsic and overriding default? *Voilà.* Therein is the metaphor for life as we can know it, if we so choose, cultivated through our spiritual practice and lots of trips to the amusement park.

Tips 63-66:
Boundaries, Velcro, Choices, and Caregiving

Tip #63: The steady and consistent practice of "letting go" during meditation, both on the cushion or mat and in the flow of regular life, is a most miraculous and beautiful process of transformation. With every release, it's as if the boundaries of your form and awareness keep expanding outward, revealing more space than was ever before imagined. My mother always told me that good parenting is all about knowing when to expand your child's boundaries. From those first scuttles around the soft walls of the playpen to a bike ride around the block to a life journey, each step of a child's growth is an introduction to new levels of space never before imagined. But it is you, the parent, who must let go of the reins a little more and a little more when you sense it is time, making parenting, once again, a brilliant example of the perfect dance of human and divine experience.

Just as you become present with your child's ever-changing boundaries, so you must be attentive to your own. By practicing loving kindness towards yourself, your spouse, your children, and other people you interact with, by expanding your boundaries in times of growth, clarity, strength and insight or bringing them in when you are in deep, raw places of emotion, meditation brings us into alignment with these needs in each moment.

Tip #64: Just when you thought it was time to teach your six-year old how to tie and untie his shoelaces, you discover that all the sneakers in Wal-Mart are made with Velcro fasteners. Zen Master Linji Lixuan said, "I have no teaching. I only untie knots."[xix] The paradox is, regardless of whether there are any teachings, or teaching to be done, we have so much to (un)learn. In parenting, we are constantly surprised at how something "tried and true" no longer applies, whether it be how to tie and untie the knots in your shoes or what your child should or should not eat. What worked for your first child may have the opposite effect on your second child. Without the open heart and beginner's mind that meditation cultivates, the dynamic world of raising children will leave you in the lurch. With an open heart, parenting is one of the most exciting and interesting experiences you'll ever be gifted. Untie the tied knots. Or just zip off the Velcro.

Tip #65: A popular teaching phrase in preschool classrooms these days is "make the right choice." If Bobby bonked Suzanne on the head and made her cry, Bobby is not a bad boy, but he did make a bad choice. Next time, since Bobby knows he is a good boy, Bobby will promise to make a good choice. I absolutely love this approach because no one is vilified, everyone is intrinsically good, everyone is empowered to choose correctly again and again, and a great foundation of loving oneself enough to want to make these good choices is paved.

Somehow, lots of us grownups missed this lesson. Maybe no one told us we actually had choices. Maybe we were branded "good" or "bad" at any given moment, at school or at home or by peers or bullies. Maybe as we got older we were overtaken by the pressure to achieve inhumane perfection in light of our society's impossibly high standards and achievement insanity, and we stopped loving ourselves. Maybe we stopped believing we were empowered to make good choices anymore. Maybe we stopped believing that we are fine just as we are. As kids get older and further away from the wholesomeness of their preschool classrooms and mother's wombs, they too forget.

In their course "Choose Again,"[xx] Diederik Wolsak and Claudette Thomas maintain that "the world you see is an outer reflection of an inner state of mind. I projected my thoughts and believed them as true. I can Choose Again. My Worth is intrinsic, unchangeable! My Worth is a given. Take a deep breath and let that in. I need do nothing to prove anything." Sure, teach your children that they can make their own choices, but by all means, embody that concept yourself. Make the choice to be peaceful and accepting, mindful and committed to the connection to Allness.

In doubt? Says the "Choose Again Toolbox": "When in doubt, choose to meditate. To meditate means to allow my thoughts to rise and fall like waves. Each thought is like a wave, which rises and then falls back into the ocean. All thoughts are meaningless; let them rise and fall and watch them disappear." So even if the only choice you make is the intention to meditate and commit to mindfulness, the results will be palpable.

Tip #66: Convention often defies instinct, whereas instinct pulls from spiritual practice. Says Meredith Garmon: "Conventional morality says:

Choose between living for yourself and caring about others. Or try somehow to hew a balance between these opposites. Conventional morality is surely wrong. Living for yourself and caring about others are not opposites." Meditation embodies this concept, and thus defines the essence of the path of the caregiver.

Tips 67-69:
Obstacles, Wisdom, and Dancing

Tip #67: There are times when you naturally feel emotional, exhausted, overwhelmed, depleted, helpless, and sometimes even hopeless, as a parent. You feel pain that is almost unbearable. It is during those times that there seems to be an exponential rise in things that "go wrong," whether it be financial crisis, emotional drama, physical illness, and more, and just when you need it the least. In her book "Break Through Your Threshold," Jai Maa[xxi] suggests that you welcome these experiences wholeheartedly by seeing them in context. Thresholds are the appearances of obstacles that will only be obstacles should you accept them as such rather than inviting them in and authentically experiencing them. Through meditation, you can sit with these obstacles until, as with all things, they cease to be, and what is next sets you free. Rumi writes often of welcoming the unwelcome, as in his famous poem "Guest House."[xxii] Mickey Singer advises you to "relax and release," and when things get "hot," notice the heat and withstand it. I've seen time and again that when you get to the other side, the magic happens, but till then, hold on and resist the temptation to panic or do anything but watch and feel. On one side you feel awful and your kids will not like it, but they will be keenly watching and learning from your handling of these very real experiences. When you do get to that other side, not only will you be "fun Mom/Dad" again, but they will have been witness to a critical life skill that is also the essence of spiritual practice.

Tip #68: Said a 98-year old wise woman to me recently: "When you are in your twenties you think you are wise because you are a grown-up. When you are in your thirties and forties you think you are wise because you have a job and kids. When you are in your fifties you think you are wise because your kids are grown up and you've got stuff. When you are in your sixties you think you are wise because you have grandkids and you have photo albums. When you are in your seventies and eighties you think you are wise because you are outliving all of your friends and you have a lot of stories about your life. But when you get to be my age you figure out that all you've been doing is defining yourself relative to other things, as if you were some kind of fixed point. That's impossible. I'm almost 100 and there is nothing to say. I'm just here, still breathing in the whole thing and I'm damn thankful for it."

TIP #69: My young son and I were watching in wonder at the early morning light illuminating the rising mists from the ground in wispy, smoky clouds. He asked me: "What is that?" I explained that it was water, changing form from liquid to vapor and going back into the air. He asked: "Why does it do that?" I dutifully told him about the water cycle, about evaporation, how the rising sun warmed the water molecules and made them dance right up into transformation. I know a lot about these things. I am a scientist, and can to this day identify almost every sea star on the planet by its taxonomic classification and geographical location.

But as I said the word "dance," I realized that he and I, in our true state of being, are no different from the rising mists of the morning. When our mind is pure and present, we too literally dance from one transformation to the next, as the forces of nature dictate. It is not our place to cling to the leaf for fear of not being dew anymore. We will only suffer unless we defer to the greater miracle before us. I know a lot about sea stars and the water cycle and ecology and biochemistry. But I never danced with them until now. I know a lot about education and taking care of kids, but without dancing with our kids we are joyless. We dance to piano lessons, to board meetings, through dishwashing, through taxes;

we dance to dance classes. We dance to the ethers, and then back again, as we are called.

Tips 70-73:
Koans, Getting Proactive, Changing the World, and Living the Dream

Tip #70: Even if you haven't been on your meditation cushion or yoga mat for weeks, you know you are doing okay when you see the mountain of laundry before you and your mind simply registers: "This is what's in front of me for taking care of in this moment." If instead your mind is saying: "WHEN WILL IT EVER EEEEEEEND?!?!" Then you have created the householder's version of a koan, worth contemplating, for there is no answer other than "Never" and "Right now," simultaneously. It's a win-win.

Tip #71: Many mornings, if you plan it right, you can still have a traditional "on the cushion" meditation practice during those precious thirty minutes right before your kids get up and start calling for their sippy cups, breakfast, clean clothes and general morning activities. If you have an area all set up, it helps—just wake up, use the bathroom, and get on the cushion. Easy, right? But the psyche doesn't make it so simple. A whole thirty minutes to yourself in the quiet? Sixty? Oh, the things you could do: get caught up on emails with a cup of coffee, fold a load of laundry, listen to your voice mails, work on your endless list of "to do's." So, how does meditation get priority status during this precious block of time? Simple: The "to do" list might get a slight dent made in it if you go that route, but it won't feel like enough time and your state of being will be instantly engaged in that hurry-up-and-do mode, setting the stage for the rest of the day and completely draining you energetically. Thirty to sixty (even five or fifteen) minutes of silent meditation will put the psyche in its place and serve to ground your entire outlook for the day.

A bonus: if you are still thinking about "all the things you could do" even while sitting on the cushion, then you have great stuff to work with during your sit. Simply watch those thoughts. Watch how you desperately want to get up off the cushion and grab your cell phone, or how you have already wandered off of counting your breaths and gotten caught up in your mental list for the day. That's proactive meditation—and even if that is all your meditation consists of this morning, it will cause a great cumulative shift within, day after day, that is worth far more than a couple more folded shirts and returned emails.

Tip #72: Life is a brilliant dance between your inner and outer worlds. By constantly freeing your soul with your daily practice via meditation and your calm surrender to your sometimes mundane duties, all the while setting your intention on what the world might need and how you can best serve it, you can become clear on your life's mission — aka your "dharma"— to effect a better future both small scale and large. Yes, folding laundry can change the world.

Tip #73: I've seen Oneness. I know all about non-duality. Used to get right to it with a twenty-five-year yoga practice and a ten-year Zen meditation practice, completely soaked in peaceful, blissful Oneness after long daily sits on the zafu cushion and heavenly sessions on the sticky mat. Now, as a working mother of two life-loving, insatiably curious and active homeschooled kids and anywhere from two to a million pets depending on the day, I am still soaked in ever-changing Oneness. I am completely One with poop, sleeplessness, noisy alarm clocks, thermometers, crashing computers, animals, in-laws, Disney movies, Nerf guns, forts, emails, dishes, laundry, Swiffers, waiting in lines, chia-seeded pancake batter and total surrender to Life as We Know It. Or, in the words of the beautiful "Hakuin's Song of Zazen":

"Our form now being no-form, in going and returning we never leave home. Our thought now being no-thought, our dancing and songs are the Voice of the Dharma.... And this very body, the body of Buddha."[xxiii] Oneness is not mine to claim, but simply is. Practice is over. We're LIVING it now, baby.

Tips 74-76:
Looking Good, Fully Being, and Labels

Tip #74: Being a meditation/yogini mom in motion is extremely good for your looks. When I show up at a class or a group sit, hair pulled back with a rubber band from an organic broccoli bunch scavenged from the bottom of a grocery bag, wearing a sweatshirt and 15-year old yoga pants that took me through two pregnancies, and notice the fashionista young ladies and elegant older women wearing impeccably matching yoga outfits and/or well-pressed white linen meditation tunics and palazzo pants with mala beads, there is only one thing to do: Fix my slump and stand/sit up straight, and relax my face. It does more for immediate appearances than any Lulululululime catalog outfit, and has the longest-term beauty benefits from within. That's probably why those elegant older women look so incredible.

Tip #75: It is when you completely lose control, that life is moving so fast through tragedy, emergency, personal crisis or the whirlwind of others whose lives are intertwined so tightly with yours that you can only be there as they dance the crazy, that your "spiritual toolbox"—all the techniques, breathing patterns, affirmations, listening techniques, koans, time to meditate, and more—are lost to you—that you have nothing left to do but just fully be in that moment and all there is to do is what's next. Scary as these times may be, they are also the closest to Grace, for in those moments you are fully being, with no luxury of distraction.

Tip #76: We as humans have such a propensity to label ourselves. For example: "I am a Mom." To take it further: "I am a Mom with three young boys." And then, with this label, we can expand to: "I am a Mom with three young boys, and that's why I am always tired." While this may seem fine in the daily workings of life, and usually what our minds default to, these very thoughts foment the fire of exhaustion and suffering. With a subtle focused shift we can go much deeper and create space for transformation. Who is the "I" telling herself that she's a mom with three boys and hence is always tired, or the busy person who is always anxious, or the artist who must always wear red, or the tortured poet, or the (insert label here)? By focusing on the "Who am I" versus all the labels the "I" is giving itself, a profound awareness begins to surface, that words can't describe. YOU are not a "mom" or a "dad" or an "overworked, under-appreciated busy person" and all the things your mind associates with it. YOU are a divine, gorgeous presence having all kinds of miraculous experiences, including parenthood and much, much more. So Hum (I am That)!

Tips 77-80:
Kensho, Clear Water, Dawn, And the Real You

Tip #77: We are already enlightened. But because we so busy taking care of others, cooking, cleaning, working jobs, trying to get a job, finding ways to shield ourselves from unpleasant things and/or creating distractions from unpleasant things, we seem to have lost sight of our natural state. That's where meditation comes in. If we meditate, we can break down the mental constructs that give us the wild notion that we can relieve our suffering by repeatedly trying to control the uncontrollable. Peace and clarity will ensue gradually, with breakthrough moments of much bigger awareness.

There are hundreds of stories of *kensho* or *Samadhi*—that grand and much-talked-about event when one sees That Which Is Bigger Than Little Me in one profound, authentic moment—and many revolve around a single turning word, sound, smell, or sight. Masters have reported reaching kensho after hearing the musical trickle of a flowing brook on Mount Fuji, witnessing the gentle opening of a cherry blossom in a temple garden, or contemplating an index finger in the dharma room.

As a parent, one is not often able to find time to contemplate a gently opening cherry blossom or go to Mount Fuji for an extended sit by a flowing brook, and thus meditating parents may feel deprived of the opportunity to experience their own proper kensho. But hear, smell, taste, feel and look around; the world you are in NOW is your doorway.

For example, one day, my kids were playing Jenga with remarkable focus. They built a looming tower out of a bunch of little pieces. Then, they giddily tried not to topple the tower over while, one by one, they pulled the pieces out. Of course, the tower tumbled. Of course, they were ecstatic, and of course, they immediately set to constructing and demolishing it again and again and again. As the tower fell down for the tenth time, the dog barked and all became so clear: we build our fragile towers, our houses of cards, to protect us from our sense of suffering and to give us a perception that we actually have control over the ancient forces all around us. To that, my kids gleefully say: HAHAHAHA! But they take it further—they also say HAHAHAHA with innocent delight while the tower is built! The tower is this life. The demolition is this life. They are inseparable on this path. And that realization is as profound as the cherry blossom, the brook, the index finger, and my children's laughter in an embarrassingly messy playroom.

Tip #78: Gurus and spiritual teachers often use a great visual aid for our true nature: a clear glass of water. Then, they add mud to the mixture to represent the self-imposed limitations of our mind, and show that while all the clear water is still in there, the mud of our monkey mind is obscuring its clarity. Time and time again I hear moms and hard-working people of all types sigh and say, in exhaustion and/or frustration: "This is just my life. My luck. This always happens to me." It's further reinforced by something like: "If I only had some more time, some more money, some more space, some more help, it would be so much easier." Instant mud. Next time these feelings and thoughts arise, and they usually do for hard-working parents and caregivers, stop for just three minutes and focus on the only things you need to get back to the clear state: your breath, your body, and the sounds and sensations of the world around you. Use your breath to filter, clean, and purify you, so that you can fully sense and experience the miracle of just being here. Clear water.

Tip #79: The power of pre-sunrise is palpable. Despite how much sleep you need and how much work that needs to be done as a parent, get to an acceptable stopping point in your work the day before, carve out some time for a nap for later in the day, and make it a priority once a week or so to wake up for your meditation at 5:15am. You will begin your meditation in the dark, cool blanket of nocturnal sounds, smells, and senses, and in the course of a short hour, while your children sleep contentedly, experience the crescendo of dawn that is nothing less than spectacular. Even if your monkey mind is running amuck, it will be impossible to deny the announcement of the coming of the Great Eastern Sun. May your day be filled with the brightness of its awakening, and set the stage for the miraculous unfolding of its very existence.

Tip #80: One really tangible technique in meditation is coming into "witness consciousness": getting behind that ever-lovin' yakking of the monkey mind to become aware of whom is really behind all of it. That "whom" is the answer to the age-old "Who am I?" Kids can totally get this concept, and it's helpful for children of all ages when dealing with feelings. Icon Mr. Rogers addressed this all the time. Sure, you ride your bike, fall down, get hurt, cry, get angry at your brother, feel like no one understands you, etc. but WHO is feeling and thinking all of these things? The real you is. The real, pure you who is all Love. My little crying son asked me yesterday: "So why do we have a mind, then?" My reply: "Your mind is a little smart monkey trying to be your friend. He is a good friend and helps us in many ways, and so we love him. He helps you add numbers and read and figure out interesting problems. But he thinks he's too important, so he also worries about every little thing and tries to make you worry with him, when really we just have to teach him that all the things going on are just part of life, and even if they don't feel good, they are okay and will pass by."

It took me several decades to first become aware of and then finally start to befriend that little monkey fella, but my son got it right away. My meditation teachings to him have been more in the way I answer his endless, eager questions, and his meditation teachings to me have been via his remarkable outlook on life. Recently, he wanted to know why bullies are so bad, why boo-boos have to hurt so much, and why big brothers sometimes pick on their littler siblings. Through this practice, we mutually understood that the bully isn't bad. The bully is a being having experiences in his life that are currently making him make bad choices. The boo-boo hurts because hurting is often a part of healing. Big brothers are, well, big brothers, and they come in all shapes and forms. I can sit on my meditation cushion and remember how to be friends with my mind and make good choices, even when the world presents bullies, boo-boos, big brothers, bills, and breakdowns.

Tips 81-83:
Space, Brooding, and Kids as Cushions

Tip #81: The most common complaint I hear (even in my own head) from parents is "there's just no SPACE in my life. How can I possibly meditate?" Life is like a ladies purse: no matter how big it is, you're gonna fill it up to the maximum with stuff. So, this "too busy to meditate" statement is really just an excuse to disguise the physics of taking up space every chance we can get. Some days are truly packed, no joke. Space, and your practice, are thus found in your concerted mindfulness in the spaces in-between. For example, when you are unpacking your groceries, instead of racing through the task to get to cooking dinner, move a tenth of a second more slowly. Take a breath between the frozen organic peas and the non-organic broccoli. Notice your reaction to the non-organic versus organic, without judgment. Notice how cold the frozen bags feel. Slow down just a fraction more. Breathe again. Notice how your ribs and belly expand outward when you inhale, creating vast space even within the busy enclosed workings of your moving, busy body. *Voilà*, space and meditation in the midst of the whirlwind.

Tip #82: Ancillary to Tip #81 is the idea that because you are very, very busy as a parent, there is thankfully little time to sit around brooding about your life, which is the meditators' biggest obstacle. If you can be okay with that, then you are really rockin' your practice. Just do what's in front of you. Then do the next thing. Pick up the Legos and dirty clothes from the floor. Change the diaper. Ground your teenager. Do your work. There is no better example of being present than that. Even if you try to brood, you will end up being too busy to let it get anywhere, and thus you will have successfully extricated a longstanding bad habit.

Tip # 83: Children are a lot like meditation cushions. They are cute and round and small, but sometimes when you are "sitting," you get impatient. You let your cell phone distract you from fully engaging. You want to go somewhere else. You feel uncomfortable and would rather eat ice cream and watch reruns of Desperate Housewives than be with that "cushion" any longer. "Sit" through all of these

sensations and feelings, just noticing them without drama, and let your kids be your cushions, metaphorically speaking. Do not sit on your children for real.

Tips 84-86:
Your Mind Phone, Phineas and Ferb, and Radical Acceptance

Tip #84: When our cell phones ring, we are like Pavlov's dogs. We could be engaged in a groundbreaking scientific discovery, or sitting with our child when he begins to sound out words and read for the first time, or attending our teenager's high school graduation during her Magnum Cum Laude speech, and when our phone rings, beeps, plays Mozart, or vibrates, we excruciatingly want to pick it up and see who's calling or texting or emailing or posting or messaging. Even if we manage to let it ring through to voicemail, we think about it for the next fifteen minutes, sitting on our hands so we won't pick it up and "just make sure it wasn't something important." This is exactly how your mind works, 24/7, with every thought.

That "stickiness" of the phone, that need and drive to always be connected to it, is the kind of unrealized relationship we have with our mind. Every thought is an intoxicating call that will not be ignored, that wants to draw you into it and carry you away. Your practice is to sit on your metaphorical hands while the thoughts ring and vibrate and beep and play Mozart, and to watch, fascinated, as your whole being reacts with fear and anxiety and worry that you might've missed something "very important," and ultimately to revel at how nice it feels to learn how to throw the whole thing into the metaphorical toilet.

Tip #85: Life as a parent means more exposure to children's and teen-oriented media than the independent cinema, edgy drama, and fine arts you were once an aficionado of. Since you are up to your ears in it anyway, find the pearls of meditative wisdom within your current situation. Here is an example: if you cannot decide what to do or where to start today because you are paralyzed with possibilities or overloaded with to-do's and worldly concerns, think of the spiritual masters Phineas and Ferb, and notice how their monkey-minded big sister Candice, obsessed only with the desire to "bust" her little brothers and win the affections of a teenage boy, compares in life enjoyment.

With openness, mindfulness, playfulness, and living in this very moment with a positive attitude, anything can happen for Phineas and Ferb (and for you), and meditation can illuminate the way. I am not sure if Phineas and Ferb meditate, but their sister would probably receive serious benefits from starting a practice. When breathing alone is as "big and awesome" as creating the biggest bounce house in the Tri-State area, when breathing alone gives you more satisfaction than busting your little brothers or winning the affections of a teenage boy, mountains move. That peace within is the answer to bringing peace at last to a monkey mind-obsessed world.

Tip #86: "Duality" is the illusion that things in life are either one way or another. Tara Brach's concept of "Radical Acceptance"[xxiv] squelches duality in one lovely term. We have lots of reasons to use "yes" and "no" throughout our parenting, professional, and personal lives. And we use them gratuitously in our mind. "Yes! I meditated/did yoga/ate healthy/used only positive words today! I rock! No, I didn't. I am doing a rotten job. Yes! My kids slept through my whole meditation and I got a full hour! No, they didn't. Yes! I mean No! I mean, yes and no, depending on how you look at it, let me think about it...." And on and on it goes in there. With one subtle but deeply profound shift in your ranting mind, all of those thoughts can be brought together by simply loving them. Yes, loving them. Doesn't matter if they are lambasting you alive. Just love them and rock them and respect them and cherish them no matter what they are doing, like a little baby in your unconditionally loving care. Welcome it all. And then, once again, fuggetaboutit.

Tips 87-90:
Not Knowing, Kid Meditation, Atoms, and Pranayama

Tip #87: One of the deepest levels of spiritual awareness is Not Knowing. There is a Zen koan that has no answer other than "I don't know!" At this point, the path reveals a great mystery: "Not knowing is most intimate." When a parent finds themselves identifying to, learning from or judging another parent in action, Not Knowing reminds us that the perception is all our own. While we can glean very much from how we perceive and process the world around us for our own path, the reality is we haven't a clue about anything or anyone else, and that willing, self-defenseless acknowledgment brings us closer to Source. We bow to the parts of our relationship to that moment that resonate with our own path, and the deep respect we give to Not Knowing. Not. Knowing. Anything.

Tip #88: In addition to not sitting on your kids, it is not necessary to ask or require them to sit, either. The Venerable Dhammajiva of the Theravada Mitirigala Nissaranavanaya Forest Monastery in Sri Lanka has noted that up until the age of six, happy, healthy children are already in full presence. They have no "samskaras," or spiritual baggage, to sit with. They are living, breathing examples of Meditation in Motion. Relationships are self-centered, though, which explains why they ask you to carry their toy car while you are lugging twelve grocery bags and a basket of laundry, or why they ask you for a twelfth peanut butter sandwich RIGHT at the moment you finally sit down to eat after serving everyone else. This age is a ripe time to teach loving kindness and compassion, to show them that there are other beings with needs besides their own. The "ahas" that arise from these teachings are cathartic and moving for both parent and child alike.

From age six and up, conditioning, world experiences, and emotions do begin to impact children, but requiring them to sit on a cushion will not train a lifetime of meditation practice in the way that requiring them to brush teeth, play piano, write thank-you notes and do homework trains them for a lifetime of good choices and self-care. Meditation must be "trained" by subtler methods, which bring the child to the cushion when he or she is ready: telling visualization stories, playing games which incorporate meditation, doing breathing exercises and yoga, being attentive to moments as they happen, and the like. The most important thing you can do to promote meditation in your children is to do regular meditation yourself. If your child just wants to mimic "Buddha" the golden retriever puppy from the Disney "Buddies" movies by making a mudra, closing his eyes, and chanting "Om" on the cushion for 30 corny seconds, by all means, let him. It may look silly, but he is mimicking an ancient practice that works, and relating to it with acceptance and fun.

Tip #89: My son recently learned about atoms, and is fascinated and enthralled with the fact that our atoms are falling off of us and swirling around us everywhere, connecting and mixing with everyone else's. He thrills in bringing me a "handful" of atoms and then taking some in return. So often we engage in our practice for ourselves, to make us feel more at ease. In many cases we can also see that our kids and spouse benefit. But the Buddha takes it much further, as he teaches in the Brahma Viharas: your practice is everyone's practice. We wish loving kindness on all beings through this practice, because we are inextricably connected to all beings past, present, and future. I recently heard an ailing friend describe herself and all individuals as "buckets, each trying not to lose their water." Indeed, when one is ill or not at ease it feels like you have to hold on to every drop you've got. But as Paramahansa Yogananda so melodically pleads: "I am the Bubble; Make me the Sea."[xxv] There are no drops. Only vast, boundless oceans and infinite quantities of atoms, all together in this present moment, falling off of us and merging with everyone else's, everywhere.

Tip #90: We often drink water just when we're thirsty, and it isn't nearly enough. I once heard a health guru give a talk who said: "if you make only one change, do this: drink water when you're NOT thirsty, and you will experience health miracles." Likewise, we tend only to breathe about half as much as we could, simply because we are breathing mindlessly, whenever there is a call for just enough air to keep us going. In yoga, the Sanskrit term "pranayama" literally means "controlling the life force," and is devoted to working with the breath for increased vitality and chi force. Mindful breathing is a moment-to-moment meditative practice unto itself. Notice the breath whenever you remember to. Notice how you breathe faster chasing after your toddler, who transforms from a snail's pace to Flash Gordon speed within seconds and whenever he feels like it. Notice how you breathe just as fast watching your sixteen-year old daughter go off to the prom with some guy named "Bull," especially while you are scaling the high school fence to keep an eye on them. If you make only one change, do this: breathe deeply and mindfully when you can under the normal circumstances of daily life, and especially when you want to breathe shallowly in a stress response, and you will experience mindfulness miracles.

Tips 91-93:
Settling in, the Cure, and Disney

Tip #91: As busy parents, it's not uncommon to treat meditation like workouts: Butt feels flabby, go to gym and do a two hour sweat buster, feel better or pull some muscles, wait two weeks, repeat. Similarly: feel uneasy or stressed, sit on the meditation cushion for two hours with mala beads and mantra music, feel better or not, wait two weeks, repeat. While it is wonderful and appropriate to heed the call of exercise and meditation when your body and mind are speaking loudly to you, they are not always instant relief for physical and mental unease. It can be quite the opposite, actually: sometimes the reactive "I gotta go do something!" the high of diving in with gusto, and the resulting letdown when expectations aren't met can have a hyperbolic effect. Better to settle in to a daily practice—a little bit in the morning and a little bit in the evening—through all kinds of internal weather, without expectation of results, but in the same way you attend to all of your other daily priorities as a routine, and enjoy the ride.

Tip #92: Continuing the exercise/meditation paradigm: just as a two-hour sweat buster won't cure three decades of a McDonald's and couch-and-TV lifestyle (to use an extreme example), neither will two hours on a cushion or even a weekend retreat cure a lifetime of mental formations and scars, known as maya and samskaras in the Yogic tradition or Mara in Buddhism. The first step in the "cure" is to let go of any idea that you need to be cured, which implies attachment to a whole mess of perceptions about yourself that are a waste of time to go back and define. The maya and samskaras will up-and-dance for you every chance they can get. Thus, your daily practice isn't to sit there and give them the Evil Eye and wish they never happened and visualize them leaving your reality with all your might and wait till you're "cured," but to dance with them right back. Like it or not, it's your life experience, so fully accept it—and then give them a loving hug as they eventually tire out and twirl out the door. There is no need to be willful about enlightenment; just dance.

Tip #93: One of the most wondrous and sometimes difficult real-life effects of a regular meditation practice is that you cultivate a remarkable sensitivity and empathy to the world around you. Great beings allow the orchestra of experience and emotion to glow through each moment, whether in a Third World country wrought by tsunamis or at a suburban theme park. Once, I took a trip with my family to the mother of all suburban theme parks—Disney World—and could feel suffering so intensely that I cried when I heard a young girl tearfully ask her determined parents why she had to wait for two hours in the hot sun to go on "It's a Small World." Later that same day, I swelled with tears of gratitude, noticing how small the world was indeed, when a non-English speaking family offered suntan lotion and smiles to an American family clearly turning beet red while waiting for Space Mountain. My daughter was dejected that we couldn't go on many rides due to the long lines, my son passed out and missed the one ride we did get on, and my husband was not at all enjoying the experience of moving along like cattle with waves of thousands of Mouse-beany-headed people. To cap off the family vacation, the AAA-recommended hotel room we booked had a clogged up toilet filled with unidentifiable unmentionables, a clogged up shower filled with the hairy parts of about 300 previous guests, and when we awoke in the morning, the bathtub from the floor above us decided to crack open through our ceiling and spill sulfur-water onto all of our belongings. I crumpled into a ball on the one remaining dry bed while my children and husband looked on, worried, with mouths agape.

The experience threw me off guard so much—an emotional breakdown at Disney?—that I spoke with my Zen teacher about the experience. If I cannot handle a supposed-to-be-fun family trip what with all the suffering even there, how do the great masters walk with equanimity and love through the trenches and stench of the most destitute slums, with thousands of starving, desperate, outstretched hands trying to get even a glimpse of nirvana? Wouldn't the collective suffering be too overwhelming, too tragic, for any mortal?

I learned that I had suffered a difficult bout of something called Zen Sickness, a term for a place in the practice in which one is an open vessel for intense joy and deep sorrow due to the compassion, awareness and overwhelming empathy being one's current state. If one has the ability and the support to get off the damp bed and stand up again, it's a beautiful moment of working with Noble Truth. Yes, the world is a piece of work. Yes, we are now fully, REALLY experiencing and feeling every last excruciating piece of it. Yes, I continue to breathe, feel, relax, watch, and allow. Yes, this effort and intention alone will help to relieve the very suffering that pummeled me. Yes, it is worth doing this practice, every last bit of it, and now I feel and know ever so keenly why. Yes. Yes. Yes.

The experience of Life is indeed a Magic Kingdom. The heart of love and gratitude that we give it is our duty and our offering.

Tips 94-96:
Vinyasa, Meditation Games, and Forest Bathing

Tip #94: A wise yoga teacher in a class I was once taking instructed us to treat our entire day like vinyasa: the practice of flowing gracefully from one pose, or activity, or act of doer-ship, to another, being fully mindful of each transition. I used this metaphor for years as a terrific mindfulness tool until one day I was faced with the following scenario: both kids were doing homework, and both wanted full attention and assistance at the exact same time. Meanwhile, the phone was ringing, the pasta was over-boiling, someone was at the door with an important delivery, and I'd just spilled a bag of shredded carrots all over the floor. All at the same time. Vinyasa? Vinyasa?!!! Unless I can figure out how to do a downward dog, camel pose, and tree pose all at the same time, vinyasa just went out the window. Sound familiar? Times like these, when our once tried-and-true models of spirituality in action seem to fail, we have two choices: 1) Do a primal scream of frustration, or 2) go deeper at that very moment into the chaos, finding vinyasa deep, deep within the micro spaces of your flailing mind, trying to smile like a champ at the whole big mess of it. Sometimes you do both, alternating, until the smile creaks through.

Tip #95: Grabbing 15-20 minutes of meditation with a three to six year old under your supervision is a bit trickier than with littler kids, who will usually be fine playing with some creative toys/coloring in a safe enclosed area, or older kids, who can be instructed to grab a great book and read for that duration of time or longer. The good old "Quiet Game" might work for about three minutes, but after a while it becomes a game of "how silly can I be to make the other person lose their cool and not be quiet anymore," which is not conducive to a successful sit. So, you must be very, very sneaky. You must tell your three to six year old that for the next fifteen minutes (great for teaching your child number progression and how to keep track of time on a clock), starting when the bell rings, he/she is on a Ninja/Power Princess challenge mission. He/she will be allowed to ring the bell. Then, wearing all black or an elaborate princess costume, the mission instructions are to move around two safe, nearby rooms carrying a magic seashell wrapped in a purple cloth. The seashell contains information which can save the world, but only if it is carried in the purple cloth for a full 15 minutes in absolute silence, touching every object in the two rooms that one can find with the cloth-wrapped shell in extreme silence, while watching the clock. At the end of 15 minutes, your child is to ring the bell once again, in order to receive the coveted Ninja/Power Princess Award Prize (of your choice: the shell is a good one) for saving the planet. This example is just one of many ways to get creative and create a win-win with your child. Truth is, by having a great sit in harmony with your child, you really ARE saving the planet.

Tip #96: We jump through many hoops just to find a way to meditate. We sign up for retreats in Bora Bora, plead with the babysitter not to cancel and then fight with traffic to get to our weekly sitting group or yoga class, tell our spouse and kids that if they don't leave you alone for twenty minutes to sit on a cushion without needing a peanut butter sandwich or help with the toilet paper that you will throw all the peanut butter and toilet paper in the trash, look on the internet at pictures of Bora Bora, wake up at 3am just to remember what a quiet moment feels like, pack up tons of toys, drawing supplies, books, and more to keep your child occupied while you try to catch a sit while supervising them, feel bad that they are sitting on their tushies watching TV at the gym child care center while you do yoga, and so on.

But achieving a peaceful state in the midst of family and busy times can be as simple as finding a forest, or just a tree. A Japanese practice called Shinrin-Yoku (forest bathing)[xxvi], developed formally in the 80's but intuitively practiced by wise seekers for millennia, is the simple act of looking at a tree, and at the most, immersing for a few hours a week in the forest. Because we are naturally and instinctively evolved to commune with the natural world, the effects are effortless and profound, much as when one spends time at the ocean. *Voilà*, a zendo you can take your family to, and all you might need is some bug spray and sunscreen.

Tips 97-99:

Sangha, Yellrap, and Your Zen Garden

Tip #97: Parents on this path go way out of their way to regularly spend time with the third jewel of the Buddha-Dharma-Sangha trio: sangha. Sangha, generally defined, is the group of kindred beings, also called Noble Friends, who share this journey with you in a mutually supportive group that takes you out of your individual wants and needs and merges you into an uplifting, synergized group energy that is totally present. Our meditation groups, chanting circles, church and synagogue congregations and fellowships, etc. are all forms of sangha.

The most natural sangha is with you every day: your family. Think of the days you are all playing tennis or soccer together, or fetch with your four-legged sangha members, or eating dinner excitedly while each member shares their day. Think about how you have no concept of yourself while you bawl when your child sings a song up on a stage. Think about how their pain is your pain, their joy is your joy, with very little separation between your self and theirs. This is total group presence, in which your individual needs and wants are dissolved in the perfect flow of this moment's experience, all together.

Tip #98: You have so many "selves," inside and out. On the outside, you are parent, spouse, recreational facilitator, academic director, counselor, chef, financial chief... the list is long. On the inside, you are what J. Tamar Stone has deemed "Selves in a Box" [xxvii]: the Commander, the Judge, the Nurturer, the Perfectionist, the Playful Child... this list is also long, and there are many books about how to learn to live with all of them. But at your deepest level you are only One You: The You that is Experiencing Living Life Right At Present (YELLRAP). That You has had many names throughout history: Narayana, Original Self, the Big

"I"... it is The You that gazes lovingly back at you in the mirror when you are ten and the same You that gazes lovingly back at you when you are sixty-five. It is the You who never leaves the Source, and it is the only You that you ever really need. The rest of the yous, the little ones that chatter around your insides and define your outsides, just make the ride colorful. Through meditation, connect with your Big You once in the morning and once at night, if even for a few moments, and watch your perspective fall into a place of Grace.

Tip #99: Your inner world is reflected in your outer world, and vice versa. That's why the Zen garden you lovingly constructed has a toy dump truck in it and American Girl spinoffs with unauthorized haircuts having a Zen rock tea party with a Perry the Platypus stuffed animal. It is not supposed to look like the Zen garden at the child-free monastery you visited in Japan. It is your Zen Family Garden, a beautiful testimonial to your path at this moment, and a metaphor for the current landscape of your inner and outer worlds. And sure, while you are constantly striving to make mindful improvements to your inner and outer worlds at each moment of each day, it is what it is each moment of each day. I bow to you, American Girl spinoffs with short hair. Rock on, Perry the Platypus.

Tips 100-102:
Meditation Techniques, the Perfect Day, and Just Enough

Tip #100: Some meditation techniques like Zen emphasize mindfulness, while others, like Theravada Buddhism, emphasize loving kindness as the most prominent focus of the practice. But ultimately, like two books of the same size holding each other up when leaned against each other, one cannot be upheld without the other. When you are mindful and attentive to what is before you in this moment, you can't help but fall in love and want to devote your entire being to that which is. When you practice loving kindness, you must be fully attentive to be authentically compassionate. Young kids are this way naturally. Notice how completely excited and passionate they get over daily experiences. Taking some time to fully engage as you play with them is one of the best forms of meditation you can muster. Yes, Legos and Teenage Mutant Ninja Turtles DO hold the secrets of the Universe.

Tip #101: One morning, in an overthought, overwrought effort to be a "mindful family," I made a plan. We would awaken together, meditate and do yoga together, cook a healthy breakfast together, garden together, make artwork together... all very peacefully and mindfully. It started out as perfectly as planned, as we all awoke together and found our meditation cushions with little problem. About two minutes later, my son said: "I want a bagel. With peanut butter." My daughter asked if she could listen to music on headphones while we meditated. I shot them both reprimanding looks, at which point they dutifully, but not joyfully, stayed quietly on their cushions, expressing their energy with tapping legs and fingers. During yoga, my daughter announced: "I like dancing better," and my son began doing "The Crane" from Karate Kid. Gardening lasted about five minutes because my son wanted to play "bug race showdown" in the dirt and my daughter got bitten by red ants. My Mindful Day was disintegrating into Something Else, and it didn't take long to understand that what I was really attempting was a Willful Day: trying to make my children, and moreover, our day, into what I willfully wanted it to be, not what was to unfold with each moment of awareness and attention to the entire family. Something Else ended up being a lot more joyful, and full of surprises, and it was easier to mindfully experience (versus sternly manage) each dynamic moment.

Tip #102: Just for this moment, I will not give in to the thought of "Not Enough"—not enough time, not enough money, not enough energy, etc. I will breathe, relax, and honor the experience of being able to have a thought of Not Enough, while letting the thought pass through. Just for this moment, I will not give in to the thought of "Too Much"—too much noise, too much mess, too much to do, etc. I will breathe, relax, and honor the experience of being able to have a thought of "Too Much," while letting the thought pass through. I will discover that with each moment of not giving in to the thought but honoring the presence that sees it, I will have "Just Enough," and everything will be fine.

Tips 103-105:
Worrying, Awakening the Buddha, and World Peace

Tip #103: I used to think that "Don't Worry; Be Happy" was a great song about the spiritual path. However, as parents, we are instinctively programmed to worry. Non-attachment is another tenet of this practice, in which we learn that the world will still go on whether we have our claws of control in it or not. There is no doubt, however, that we must maintain a certain amount of both control and worry when it comes to our kids if we are to be responsible parents. While this may seem contradictory on one level, it actually provides a great way to get to the deeper levels of peace, non-attachment, and connection to Source.

Here's a great example: one great mother I know, Kayla, had regular anxiety attacks over the "what if's": What if something happened to me? What would become of my kids? What if one of my children fell ill or got seriously hurt? What if we can't make enough money to take care of our kids?" Etc. Her deep commitment to their well-being and feeling of not being able to control certain things were robbing her of her peace of mind. Her practice? Every time the thoughts and feelings arose, she tried to remember not to let them spiral outward, but rather to sit and just notice them. She noticed where she felt sensations in her body. She noticed WHO was feeling and thinking and worrying. When her mind told her to get back into thinking and solving and worrying, she lovingly told it "no, it won't work, but thanks for trying to help," as she would to her own child. Over time, she still worried about their safety and happiness, but from a more grounded and reasonable perspective in proportion to life as it was. She did everything she could to provide for their needs, but she did not spiral into hyper-anxiety. Her kids benefitted from her better state of mind. My new title for the famous song? "You'll Probably Worry; But You Can Still be Happy."

Tip #104: The Zen Kanzeon (Compassion) Sutra, a standard in the Zen tradition, is a perfect testament to living meditation: "Absorbing world sounds awakens a Buddha right here! This Buddha, the source of compassion; this Buddha receives only compassion. Buddha, Dharma, Sangha, just compassion... moment after moment the true heart arises.... Time after time there is nothing but THIS."[xxviii] In "The Untethered Soul," Michael Singer invites you to "wake up" whenever you hear a worldly sound: the telephone, the doorbell, the cry of your baby, the squawk of your pet parakeet, the voice of your teen saying "whatever." With the ring of the 6am alarm, the beep of the computer, at the playground, in Disney World, at a birthday party, and beyond, there are many shining opportunities to awaken your Buddha, right here, right now.

Tip #105: One hour of news is enough to put one over the edge of hopelessness: wars, genocide, ecological destruction, suicide. We cannot accomplish peace—peace for the world, peace for oneself, peace for your loved ones, peace for all beings—without peace within. Meditate. We cannot support others in achieving inner and outer peace without compassion. Practice loving kindness. Start with your children, your spouse, your immediate relationships as your springboards of eternal Love. One person's sincere practice is the world's boundless benefit. There is a way.

Tips 106-108:
PB&J's, Mountain Climbing, and Divine Parenting

Tip #106: There will come a point when peanut butter and jelly sandwiches will take over your life. About every two hours or so, your son-on-a-growth spurt will holler: "Mom, may I please have a PB and J? On Italian bread? With the crusts taken off?" Dutifully, you schlep to the kitchen and slather the goods onto two GMO-free slices of bread, remove the crusts, cut them into triangles or squares, and deliver the result with a glass of water. This will continue for about five years, three times a day, until you realize that your son is plenty big enough to make it for his own darn self.

Before this liberating realization arrives, however, endless PB & J prep is a great opportunity to practice "Beginner's Mind." To wit: As you begin your 42,347th sandwich according to linear time, remember that the only moment that actually exists is THIS one, separate from a concept of worldly time, and the experience of this moment is to be fully realized as if it is for the very first time. Slow down and experience every step of the sandwich-making process by appreciating how your mind can recognize the ingredients and control your muscles to open the jars and skillfully spread the gooey sauces. The miracle of this moment is brilliantly demonstrated with one sandwich, the only sandwich that matters right now. If you can consciously avoid the trappings of the veteran mom mind, kvetching "here I go again," you will exist with every sandwich request as an enlightened being.

Tip #107: There is a familiar stereotype of the earnest and determined spiritual seeker climbing the rugged, slippery mountain while fighting blizzards and wayward vultures along the way, to get to the Guru sitting at the top. Once there, the Truth is discovered. We are no different; our mountain simply consists of dishes, diapers, laundry, schedules, jobs, bills, and general householding and worldly experiences, and our blizzards and vultures come in the form of our mind trying like the dickens to convince us that we are not living in the perfection of Oneness right now. Put your coat on and climb that mountain. You'll know when you're at the top, and it's usually when we've forgotten that we were even trying to get to a concept of one.

Tip #108: The Great Vow of the Bodhisattva Earth-Treasury claims that one's personal enlightenment is not complete "till all have achieved the Ultimate Liberation." To continue:

> *"As long as space endures,*
> *As long as sentient beings dwell,*
> *Until then, may I too remain to dispel*
> *the miseries of all sentient beings."* [xxix]

There are hundreds of similar vows throughout the spiritual literature from many traditions worldwide. So, whether you consider your meditation practice "successful" or not, whether you manage to sit daily in perfect harmony with your little Buddha children or still scramble to catch a few minutes of peace now and then while your kids climb up the bookshelves, one thing is clear: Your practice is the world's practice, and we are all Divine Mothers and Fathers to each other. Treat each other well.

PARENT STORIES

Got sangha? The Buddha declared "sangha"—the community of kindred spirits supporting each other along the Way—as one of the three jewels, as important as the Source we are all seeking (Buddha Nature, Allness, Suchness, True Self, Narayana, Holy Spirit, Mana, and the myriad of other names from worldwide traditions that apply), and the way we live in the world making good choices (Dharma). As proclaimed in the Chant of Boundless Compassion[xxx], it's the world itself, and the compassion we have for ourselves and others in each and every moment of everyday experience, that brings us to enlightenment:

Absorbing world sounds awakens a Buddha right here!
This Buddha, the source of compassion
This Buddha receives only compassion
Buddha, Dharma, Sangha, just compassion
Thus the pure heart always rejoices
In the light recall this
In the dark recall this
Moment after moment the pure heart arises
Time after time there is nothing but THIS!

Well, there are no shortage of world sounds to absorb in the world of parenting, and they seem to exist in full expression during most of your everyday moments as your six year old gleefully runs out of the bathroom naked singing "We're off to see the Wizard!" at a higher decibel level than your six-month old screaming for milk, or your sixteen year old slamming her door. There are indeed lots of opportunities to practice dharma in these moments and try to make good choices. But what of sangha? Do you really share a lot in common with the soccer dad who just sucker-punched the coach for not letting his kid be the goalie, or the theater/dance mom who plasters head shots of her makeup-laden child all over social media and posts "dish" on the latest Hollywood scandals?

In short, yes and yes. As your practice deepens, you begin to see only connection with others, not separation. Compassion and love become abiding principles. But along the way, it *is* nice to connect with parents who are maintaining some kind of meditation practice, others who share a common value and intention of living in mindfulness and loving kindness in some way. They're out there—and once you start looking for them you realize there are more than just a few. These parents are your next closest sangha, right after your family. And their stories are diverse, poignant, and true. Here are just a few of my fellow parent sangha members, which by default and kindred nature, are yours too.

Kiona: Seeing Your Child

Kiona is a mindful parent with two very bright kids, ages seven and nine. She and her husband Raj are both physicians with very full schedules, and their kids are involved in piano, tennis, gymnastics, plays, and more, all while maintaining good grades and great attitudes. Kiona's mindfulness practice before family life was not formal. "I came from a Mormon background. Dove deep into the secular world once I left the church in my late teens, then realized I needed some spiritual support once I had kids. Lots of fodder for spiritual growth there!" Kiona has looked to the teachings of Pema Chodron as well as contemporary mindfulness practices.

"Parenting is a really good vehicle for spiritual growth. It's a good edge to walk. Mindfulness is the ability to REALLY see what's happening in the moment, as it is. I come from it from a psychological standpoint. We have so many experiences from our childhood that were formatively traumatic, a lot of stored stuff that clouds the way we see our children rather than seeing how our children are, fresh. So when you start to quiet or address attachments happening within yourself, it gives you perspective about what is actually happening. Stuff that happens in your past makes you catastrophize the future. Mindfulness clears or separates stuff from the past so your child can grow in real time. This isn't a do-over. Your childhood is done. It's their turn. Give it to them."

Kiona shared some real-life examples of how mindfulness helped her resolve some very stressful events with her children. "My daughter is a really intense kid, and she can have big emotions. She was one of those toddlers that from ages eighteen months to about three and a half would have ten to fifteen tantrums per day. She was my first child, and I had no idea what to do. I was so inconsistent—I would get angry, ignore her, give in—everything, anything, to prevent the tantrums. Then I started mindfulness therapy for myself. There, I remembered that in my family growing up we were always supposed to be happy. If I got sad, my mom got worried. If I got angry, my dad got really angry. There was a lot of pressure to be happy all the time. So, through mindfulness, I was able to connect to that three-year old inside who wanted to cry. I was trying to correct that same little girl in my daughter, trying to quash her emotions. Once I realized that I could let her connect to those emotions, those feelings which were very real for her in those moments, I could empathize with her. I could tell her that I saw she was upset and be there with her. So connecting to that past part of me, identifying it, helped me get clear to Lia, rather than projecting my old self. My practice isn't to get rid of it; that "stuff" is still there, but it's not all jumbled up together with what's happening now."

In addition to mindfulness training, Kiona read meditation books, and connected to the idea of impermanence. "I would say: 'Lia's crying, and she will not cry forever.' That really helped. My mind was saying all kinds of stuff: 'this will lead to all kinds of things, like her not being able to take pressure and not getting into college, etc.' But mindfulness made me understand that she is just crying, and it will pass. You ride the wave."

With awareness, Kiona acknowledges that this path can be used to curb potentially destructive situations. "I learned that as a parent, my biggest problem was anger. I would just explode. I yelled, spanked, and could really scare my kids in my burst of anger. I am still not proud of this, but I learned by mindfully watching this tendency that the lead-up to the explosion was two hours in the making. When I am aware of it in myself, I learn time and again that it all has to do with my own behavior, not my child's. Now it is so much easier to intervene during the hours before the explosion, like feeding your toddler before his hunger makes him out of control. You don't use mindfulness to control the explosion. You use it to head it off at the pass."

So what if you don't head it off at the pass and end up exploding after all? Watch and learn, and love and have faith in yourself, and communicate to your kids. It's a gradual process, and each step counts, no matter what happens. Kiona's family has reaped great benefits as a result.

Sabrina: The Bigger Picture

Sabrina is a warm, loving mom of two precocious children, and a great example of a parent who had a longstanding yoga and meditation practice years before she had children. She was raised in California in a churchgoing family, but during business trips to north Florida as a very young adult she attended dharma talks by Michael Singer at the Temple of the Universe and almost immediately changed her spiritual leanings to a more Eastern basis. Over the years, she began a long distance relationship with a Florida man who was a Temple regular, married him and moved to a property on Temple grounds. She discovered that the yogic teachings she was receiving at the Temple resonated with her life's path and vision much more than her Sunday church visits ever did, and she adopted this path as a way of life. "I fell in love with yoga head over heels. It was like I jumped in the water all at once and found that I was actually a fish and was supposed to be in water the whole time. I was so happy that I did it—I never questioned the path."

At the age of thirty, the longing for a baby hit hard, and soon afterwards, she and her husband were expecting. Speaking of expecting, "we just expected and understood that the baby would be raised in our yogic environment: vegetarian, mindful, etc.—basically the same lifestyle we had been practicing for years, just add kids." But having a baby proved more challenging—er—growthful—than she had anticipated. "I was used to being in control over things in my life and work, and generally felt self-empowered even in challenging times through my spiritual practice. The baby changed all that. I felt powerless for the first six months. When the baby cried, I didn't have anything I could fix. I just had to learn how to let go of wanting to control things to fit the vision of how I wanted the baby to be: not crying, sleeping well, eating healthy, and all the other 'shoulds.' By the time he was one to two years old he still had needs, but it got a lot easier. In reflection I think I was causing some of this with my inability to control things; me not relaxing was causing him not to relax. Me not perceiving reality as it really was made reality different and difficult for me."

When Sabrina went back to her high-powered job, new challenges arose. "Work was always my outlet, even my distraction, when I was working from home and needed to get in control of something. But when I went back to the office and a nanny was taking care of the baby, I was torn: should I be at work, or should I be at home? There was this whole period of me wanting to match my preconceived notions, a lot of me listening to my mind and all my 'shoulds.' The energy of the emotions behind that was so strong that I'd forget my mindfulness/yoga practices. Every time other things came up, I naturally went to my training in mindfulness. But not for the baby. For the baby, my mind sometimes just took over. That was my samskara, my thing to work through. In the perfection of the Universe I got what I got: my son was not going to cooperate, not be soothed, not eat what I wanted him to eat, not be nice to strangers, not give me an easy out. But my grounding was in the understanding that I am part of a bigger thing—not my mind, not my emotions, but the one who sees these things—and this knowledge helped my mind start to see things more logically. I turned to an intellectual view of the teachings as a first step, to use my mind to get me out of it and back to an experiential understanding."

Sabrina's spiritual teachings made her keenly aware that her mind could be used as a way out of her mind, by wrapping around the parts of the concepts that the mind could see. "I am. I am the Big I. I am the Witness. Thoughts are things. I am the Experiencer." These and other tools that resonate with you can help you remember your way out when you get stuck. It might not happen quickly, but it happens if you persevere with intention and purpose in your practice, and withstand the discomfort as it arises, over and over again.

"Little by little, bit by bit, I started to relax and see things as nothing different than anything else put in front of me, no matter what the mind says. Thoughts and emotions aren't real. It's just energy—intense energy, but just energy—moving through you. It doesn't make it holy if I get my son to eat carrots, at least not holier than any other thought. I am not saying I am perfect with this, but I treated my role as 'mother' from that perspective: not my thoughts, but from love and serving what is in front of me with that love. My intention was always focused on letting go—it is kind of an undercurrent running through partly because of the prior years of practice in everything big and small prior to that. So I treat motherhood the same way—it is just sometimes big stuff to let go of so it takes more chipping away. Prior to that (and since kids) big stuff can happen at work, relationships, whatever. But with kids, for me it feels like it takes more effort sometimes because my mind says: THIS—this is important!!!! You can't do... or you should do..."

Sometimes, that means accepting things that she would like to see happen differently, in favor of a bigger and more balanced picture. "My son is thirteen now, and so with his cell phone, I consented to let him walk around the mall separately from me for awhile. He returned later, proudly enjoying junk food purchased with his own money, which would not have been my choice. I felt the urge to react, but instead made a conscious decision to relax and approach him from the perspective of love and awareness of the parts of the experience that did resonate with me, like his obvious pride in his growing independence, which was the bigger thing that was happening." Sabrina uses her mindfulness practice to see a whole picture, rather than just the parts that really hit her "stuff" and make her want to react.

Mark: Bringing It Home

As a dharma/meditation teacher in the Tibetan tradition and a father of six, Mark Winwood is no stranger to everyday family life, and as is the case with many who have become teachers, his very seeking for a deeper purpose in the face of suffering brought him to not only embrace a path of meditation, but now to teach bi-coastally via an endeavor geared specifically for house-holding Americans, called The Chenrezig Project (www.chenrezigproject.org).

"I was raised in New York City with no spiritual or religious upbringing, but I was bar mitzvah'd at the age of thirteen because that's what all my friends did in Queens. I didn't understand anything the Rabbi told me to say, and didn't do or feel anything Jewish-related afterwards.

"When I was nineteen, I graduated from high school and hitchhiked with a friend to California. It was 1971, there was a lot happening during that time, and I wanted to see it for myself and learn. This was my first time on my own, away from home. New York was a fantastic place to grow up, but there was so much to experience, especially on the West Coast. I met lots of different sorts of people, was introduced to psychedelic experiences, lived for a while in a 'squatters' rights' commune deep in the Mendocino forest and was introduced to a creative world of writings from different authors, including those of Ram Dass, who had just published *Be Here Now*.

"Lots of different experiences, and through it all I became aware that there was infinitely more going on in life than I had been led to believe; the whole world opened up in brilliant possibility. That was my beginning of a sense of something more, something you might call 'spiritual.'"

Mark returned to New York for college and settled into a more standard lifestyle. "But there was this thing that had awakened in me, and soon I was watching the *Village Voice* to learn of Eastern teachers that were coming to Manhattan. I had no idea of the specifics of Buddhism, Sufism, Hinduism, Taoism, or anything else prior to this, but the teachings I was hearing were in line with what I'd experienced out West, and believed to be true."

Nonetheless, life became traditional. Mark graduated, got a solid job, married, and had three children. "I was still in Queens, and was very involved in family and child-raising. But now and then I would go listen to a teacher, a lama, a monk. I was always picking up books, keeping a finger in that world, but it wasn't a huge part of my life. I was becoming a self-important executive with a prestigious job and demanding responsibilities. Sadly, I created the conditions that brought an end through divorce to that marriage."

Eventually, Mark got married a second time and moved to Florida, where he had three more children. "I became a New York-to-Florida commuter, trying to split time between my two families. The second marriage was never solid because I was never really there enough, in body or in mind. Working, being on airplanes constantly, and trying to support two families... impossible to do well... stress, stress, stress. Looking back, I was lucky it didn't kill me.

"We struggled along, but that marriage eventually fell apart. At that point I saw everything, just everything I had and wanted going away, lost... and something about what I was exposed to in the past hit me. Right then, at the age of fifty-two, I recreated the spirit of the California trip... I packed a backpack and went to India. Always curious, I wanted to be in the Himalayas, far away, in a place like that. I had no idea what if anything, I was looking for. I just needed to go."

He stayed in India for three months, touring a bit and being drawn to the Tibetan communities in the North. It was in one of these communities that he became friends with a Tibetan man, a one-time monk who was living in India after having spent years in a Chinese prison in Tibet for possessing photos of the Dalai Lama.

"Singhi and I became fast friends, and no longer was I simply a tourist, but a family friend. Singhi, his brother and I spent weeks of evenings talking about the story of their imprisonment and subsequent escape over the high mountains and into India, with me writing their story aided by constant look-ups in a worn Tibetan-English dictionary.

"And it was there, through those nights and in the midst of Singhi's family and friends, those remarkable people, that I found what I didn't know I was looking for: There was this deep grace about these Tibetan people... a beauty, fearlessness, generosity and kindness that was so intuitive, so natural. Living as refugees in a third world country was so difficult, so full of uncertainty and hardship. There I was as the American traveler with a Swiss army watch, $100 sneakers and credit cards in my wallet, and I saw this part of me that was this hungry, self-obsessed creature next to them. It was undeniable. I saw it so clearly. It hit me so hard."

Upon returning to America, Mark knew that a change-of-direction door had opened in him that would affect him forever. "A friend asked me: 'So you finally got that India stuff out of your system?' to which I replied: 'No, I've just discovered something that I don't yet fully understand, and I'm going back.'" Three months later, he was again on a plane to India, where he volunteered to teach conversational English to Tibetan refugees.

That's when he discovered that deeply ingrained cultural Buddhist sensibilities and inclinations were at the core of why these Tibetan people were as they are. "Buddhism for them is not like a religion where you practice on Sundays and holidays, but an intrinsic part of how they see and live in the world with generosity, patience, kindness, and that's what I wanted to learn for myself."

While still in India he went on an intense two-week Buddhist retreat where "I was exposed to many of the 'ground rules' as well as learning how and why we meditate. At the retreat's end I spoke to one of the teachers, explaining my dilemma: I needed to go back to Central Florida where my young children were, but this Buddhism was so precious and there was nothing like it there. Her response: 'Take it back, and show it and share it with others.' And that's how the Chenrezig Project began in the U.S."

Mark became an established teacher back in Florida while, as a divorced weekend dad, he worked to co-raise his second set of children. He noticed how his new perspectives, cultivated by his continuing deep studies of Buddhism and his meditation practice, affected his relationships with all of his kids. "My second son was born with Down's Syndrome twenty-four years ago. Before I was on this path, I would walk him in his stroller and see the looks of many people just staring at him, and I'd get angry. I would say 'F-You, what are you looking at?' to them in my mind as they gawked. But after being introduced to the Buddhist perspectives and experiencing the effects of embracing these perspectives enhanced by my meditation practice, I became keenly aware of the self-created suffering of all beings, and that awareness brought out an understanding that kept me from being angry at the gawkers any longer. It was their pain, their ignorance; it wasn't about me or my son. And from that understanding began to rise empathy . . . and compassion. This practice helps us understand the world not just from the self-cherishing aspect of 'me, myself and I,' but from vast, much broader, other-regarding points of view."

Mark feels that the relationships with all of his kids have benefitted in different ways from his later-in-life meditation practice and compassionate teachings, but he never taught them meditation or Tibetan Buddhism directly. "I was very different from any of their friends' dads, but rather than being strange or weird, it was all kind of cool and interesting to them. They became familiar with my perspectives not by me doing any proselytizing, but simply by the osmosis of living. In my home there were lots of things from Asia all around that they were exposed to and became familiar with, and when they brought friends over I found my kids function as mini-museum guides, touring their friends throughout the house, explaining everything, such as who the Dalai Lama is, the purpose of Tibetan prayer flags and what's really being seen in those Thangkas hanging on the walls.

"As parents, it's a wonderful calling to plant seeds in our kids' minds which will one day blossom into those wonderful attitudes I saw in the Tibetan people. For kids, it's not about indoctrinating them to teachings or dogma—not too many teenagers want to hear about impermanence—but when they see you live with compassion and kindness and generosity and they connect with that, something quite beautifully human occurs."

Mark believes that his practices have had a particular impact on his relationship with his oldest son, who is a budding yogi, musician and meditator. "He felt betrayed and was completely furious with me after the divorce, and our relationship suffered greatly. But we're now as good as we've been for a long time. I knew the things I was exploring resonated with him, but he pushed them away for a long time because he associated them with me. But these views and practices, and in particular meditation, teach us that everything is merely occurring, always changing, and with that we must be patient and allow things to happen. As they do, we realize opportunities are always arising and begin to recognize them when they do, and then as mindfully and skillfully as we can, we use them for benefit and virtue . . . for whomever is walking toward us as well as ourselves. From this side, engagement in this has really enriched the fabric of our relationship. I don't know where we'd be now if not for these practices."

Mark illustrates through his life and relationships that everything we encounter is grist for the mill of our spiritual practice. "By working to cultivate awareness of what's occurring in our mind at all times, and then being mindful of how that relates to the spiritual path we're walking, we stop feeding the hungry 'me-ness' of mind. And as meditation shows us how to embrace what is arising in our mind and not rush toward or push thoughts away, our life off the cushion, as parents, friends, workers, as simple human beings, can be one of great meaning and well-being."

Mark illustrates through his life and relationships that the world is our practice. By not feeding the mind, by opening to every moment time and again, by not rushing towards or pushing things away, life can unfold. Your only job—in fact, the great gift we are given—is the choice we can make to embrace each experience. Meditation cultivates the ability to embrace the gift each moment brings, first once in a while, and eventually as your default state, to the benefit of all. Mark likens it to a computer: "When you meditate, this clarity, strength and perspective becomes part of your internal operating system . . . active within and for everything you do."

He continues: "Meditation cultivates the ability to embrace and nurture the fertility of each moment. At first this occurs occasionally, and then as our practice deepens and becomes habitual, this becomes more and more your default state, to the benefit of all."

Bob: Be In Their World

Bob is a loving grandfather with a wide-open heart, a strong but warm presence, and a student of meditation and yoga. In the early years of his fatherhood, he was an absent parent due to a demanding and travel-oriented work schedule and a chronic battle with addictions, but by the time his three children were in their tweens and teens, a rising consciousness within him changed his parenting approach and he became more available to his kids physically and emotionally. "I was grateful to have a do-over before they got much older. If I didn't take the time to listen to this inner voice and do meditation and spiritual healing, I would have lost my effectiveness in life, and particularly as a parent. I once thought that I couldn't get everything done, but then I started to realize that anything's possible—except when I say it's not." Today, he has a close relationship with his adult children, with open conversations, love, and sharing, and two of his kids have modeled his spiritual path in their own lives.

Bob's daughter recently had a crisis in her own life. "I was able to be there for her. Really there—mindful, present, and able to set aside the things that were always needing to be done and the things that really *matter.*" In another example of this mindful relationship practice with his adult children, Bob cites his youngest child: "She's in a type of marriage that dictates that the man is the head of the household. It works for her, but not for me, intellectually. But I can now accept it. If I had a yoga metaphor for this perspective, I'd call it 'staying on my own mat.'"

But Bob's grandchildren are the ones who are really reaping the benefits of his later-in-life transformation, derived from meditation and spiritual practice. His oldest grandchild is autistic, and from the grounded, present perspective that Bob's practice brings, he is able to be more attentive to his grandson's needs. "Most importantly," says Bob, "I can love him right where he is NOW. It's so much easier for me to do that than before. He teaches me a lot. His spiritual practice is all love, and he and all my grandchildren love me so much. It's all love."

Bob has specific advice for parents and grandparents: "Be in their world. Be present physically, of course, but really *be* with them. When my granddaughter was five, I read books in her classroom, and continued to do so until she was in 4th grade, five or six times a year. I did the same with my grandsons, and would have done it with my children. Express your love. Don't hide it. Practice your patience. Be the Loving Self in *their* world."

Jeff: Breaking a Chain

Jeff is a kind, grandfatherly man who can give hope to any parent who might think it's "too late" to start a mindfulness practice. Meditation allowed him to get out of the anger he felt from his past, and create space in the present moments for love to come through.

"My childhood was a disaster. My parenthood was too. I didn't get to raise my daughter, and as a result, I never got to have the kind of relationship I wanted to have with her. She has a step-dad, and on family gatherings like Christmas, I would listen to her talk about how her dad is going to help her with this or that, and I knew she was talking about her step-dad, not me. I had to teach myself how to deal with that, with the hurt. I had to be taught. I had to learn through mindfulness meditation that today my reward is the experience of today. And now I can teach my grandchildren—her kids—where to really find happiness. Best of all, I have a lot to offer them *because* of the mistakes I've made, which gives me a lot of gratitude. You do this practice for relationship. You don't do it to try to create the 'perfect' family. You do it to create relationships of love and acceptance. It is never too late to stop and learn along the way. The reward is in my heart: I get to be the grandpa I want to be, instead of the angry, hurting person I used to be."

Through mindfulness meditation, Jeff effected transformation. In doing so, he broke a chain of hurt that had lasted for generations.

Emily and Greg: Nurture and Nature

Emily and Greg are talented and successful architects in San Francisco, and parents to ten-year old Marco, who attends a Chinese-American school. Emily, born in Taiwan, comes from a very traditional Chinese family that is Buddhist more by generations-long default rather than recent seeking or formal sitting practice, while Greg, as a Japanese-American born in Hawaii, was raised in a more typical American household with no particular self-label. As individuals, they are very different not only culturally, but in personality as well. In their core attributes related to work, parenting, and the integration of mindfulness, however, they are remarkably similar. They focus on both their similarities and differences with each other in their relationship as a core tenet of their parenting.

Emily observes that modern society has become so partitioned, and people end up wearing so many hats, that our thinking is not integrated into a whole picture of life anymore. "We want our kids to excel, to do better than us, but we water down life for them in all its little parts rather than showing life to them as it is. The problem I see a lot in parenting and life in general is that we get too cerebral, and everything just becomes doing—do this, do that. In Architecture School, my professor said that the quality of a design project proposal is not equivalent to the amount of energy or calories you put into it. A lot of students thought that by making things more difficult for themselves in terms of sweat and energy, the better the project would be. 'If I am busier, I am better.' Our minds convince us of this, and this is the way modern society has become, even though it makes no sense to me anymore."

She continues: "All our lives, we are told that it's all about nurture, not nature. I wanted to believe that, and tried to do all the things we are told we are supposed to do, but when Marco was born, nature and instincts kicked in. I had to learn how to trust my gut and not let my buttons—or his or Greg's—get pushed by all the 'shoulds.' That's mindfulness—trying to 'mind' who he really is, and who I really am, and trying to communicate with each other from this perspective. He is ten now, and now I'm learning how to let go, to be more sensitive to him, not baby him as much as I want to, even though I miss those days. I have to change as he changes, not hold on."

Greg pipes in: "This path is about teamwork when you are in a family. It's about balance, because we're not always simpatico when it comes to parenting, so there's a lot of letting go there, too. I can't hold fast to my opinions and I have to communicate well and try to do it in a respectful way. Our backgrounds and our parents are very different. My family was more American, and in the seventies in Hawaii when I was a kid, my mom was a very liberal teacher. Her approach was more experimental, whereas Emily's parents were more old school Chinese and very traditional."

As different as they are, mindfulness as a way of life permeated both of their lives since childhood, and this ingrained mindfulness has brought consistency to their parenting. "There is definitely stress, and there is disagreement," says Emily. "But we are aware when it happens and so we put our mindfulness practice on communication, respect, and consistency so we don't get caught up in our differences, but rather use them to strengthen us. We can show Marco that we are thoughtful of each other, not just caught up in this or that."

Greg said: "One thing I used to say when Marco was an infant was 'Happy Mother, Happy Child.' It seems like people focus on what they think the child needs to the point that they themselves become unhappy, so everyone needs to be involved to get happy. There needs to be compassion, for everyone, not just one at the expense of the other. This applies to other relationships as well, like work relationships. I had an experience just the other day in the Billing Department, with a very frustrating client. My practice kicked in and instead of reacting, I bit my tongue, worked on my compassion and tried to see it from her point of view. That made it possible to talk to her and work out our issues. It's the same in a family. And Marco learns to be compassionate of us as well."

Emily concurs: "Open communication brings compassion and trust. If our mind gets in the way and we start making all these assumptions, like 'oh, my child will never understand this, or my husband just won't get it,' then someone will be left unhappy and misunderstood. This path is all about relationships, and compassion, and not suffering."

The point Greg and Emily make about happiness all around versus parenting through sweat equity is a central point of this book. Parents rationalize putting off their personal meditation practice so they can put everything energetically into parenting—as modern society will happily dictate through magazines, media, peer pressure and more—without realizing that their meditation practice, in whatever form it takes, is the most energetically efficient way to accomplish this task, alleviating suffering for all at the expense of none.

Hanan and Erin: Gratitude and Purpose

Hanan and Erin are sisters-in-law married to two brothers of Canadian-Egyptian descent. As practicing Suni Muslims, mindfulness is a family affair, as both families live next to each other, engage in their practice formally five times a day, and integrate their mindfulness principles into their daily family life. Often operating as a single, two-mother unit, life with Hanan's three kids Adam (9), Mariam (7), and Selma (3), and Erin's four children Anwar (12), Hamza (8), Yasin (6) and Malik (2) is anything but quiet and meditative. On the contrary: the children are animated, active, expressive and exuberant. But it is clear that Hanan, Erin, and their families are on a unified, purposeful path that is reflected in daily life, and that this path encompasses the same principles of mindfulness that we have seen throughout this book.

Both mothers were devoted Muslims before becoming parents, Hanan since childhood in Egypt, and Erin since about the age of twenty, when as an American in Michigan discovered that the practices resonated with her as "a way to make life easier. It's like a guide for life." Very generally speaking, it involves dedicated, mindful prayer five times per day. Says Erin: "It's hard to pray five times a day, to set aside time to remember what and how your life is supposed to be, where it is supposed to be going, but it's so important."

Hanan adds: "And to be a better person, to be a good person, and be good to others."

Erin continues: "We do this to commit to staying on a straight path. There are a lot of things involved—rituals, different kinds of prayers for different things, etc."

"But the general idea," Hanan says, "is that this practice always brings you back to what's really happening, in a direct way. It's a time that we intentionally put aside to remember that life is not in your control. It reminds us to feel gratitude; that's a large part of it. We can also ask for help, support, whatever is needed. The practice brings peace, relief, and happiness, and afterwards there is a sense that life is really okay. It's only five to ten minutes each time, but it gives us perspective."

Now that Hanan and Erin are moms, this daily practice is kid-inclusive. Hanan notes that "all of the kids are encouraged to practice. The older kids are required to do it. The younger kids get exposure and encouragement, and they can see how the practice makes us better at dealing with problems and such."

Erin says: "Everything that happens to us in life is considered a test. You can either let it go and grow from it or be dragged down by it. Once you practice enough and get used to looking at things, you can do that in each moment."

"Right," says Hanan. "You learn to look at things on an individual basis. So when something happens to you, that's your test, your opportunity to let go. Take my daughter Mariam. She was born with a heart condition, but I didn't know this until eighteen hours after her birth. She had open heart surgery when she was two weeks old, and I had very strong emotions. I would've broken down, asked 'why me?' But then I turned to my practice, and asked myself: 'how am I going to handle this and grow?' It grounded me. I remembered that I am not ever given more than I can handle, and so I knew I was given Mariam because I could handle the situation. She was my gift."

Erin agrees. "You need to prepare yourself for what life brings, and what your reaction might be. Our practice does that. It's easier for Hanan because she's been practicing longer, but I know that it also really helps with the little stuff, like all the things we have to do all the time, every day, as moms."

Hanan continues: "To control anger and frustration at all the little things you have to deal with is where it really helps. It's a constant calming, a constant coming to your center. You're out there doing all the little minute things and can get all stressed out about it, and forget the very miracle that you have eyesight and breathing. The practice keeps you in a positive state because you are so thankful. People around you are running around saying 'I'm late, I'm late!' and are so stressed. But with this practice there is a constant reminder that it's not all about you. It's much bigger than that."

Erin relates a story about distraction. "Sometimes all those things distract us from what's really important if we aren't mindful. There's a great story about a person who is stuck in a well. There are alligators at the bottom and a hungry lion at the top, so this person has some big things to deal with. But the person sees a little dot of honey on the wall right in front of him. Instead of moving forward to face the very real and large situation he is in, he just eats the honey to put off dealing with it even longer. That's the human way without this practice, to keep distracting oneself from whatever it is they fear or do not want to deal with because it is so big. And a lot of people do this because they cannot forgive themselves or others. The best is when you can forgive right during moments of anger or pain."

"Yes, a big part of this practice is forgiveness," adds Hanan. And mindfulness is all the time, not just five times a day for five or ten minutes each time. The five times are to reboot, to start again, to remember that it's about this moment, to ask for help if we need it, to remember that life is about purpose, to feel gratitude, and to serve and help others. It grounds me as a parent and it gives my kids a sense of grounding and purpose."

Jeanette: Life Is Your Child

Jeanette is a vibrant, funny, single, middle-aged woman with a beautiful motherly presence and no children. "I never gave birth to any children, and at this late age never will. My 'children' are the little munchkins of friends and now—at this age—grandchildren of friends, co-workers and friends whom I nurture, daily inspirational text messages sent to a long roster of folks, acts of kindness done to strangers and customers/patients, and caring for my favorite 'kid,' Joey the Wonder Dog."

Jeanette laughs heartily and does not hesitate to cry when moved deeply. She is a caregiver by nature, both in her work as a speech therapist and in her personal life as one who makes her friends as family, seeing to their needs and helping out in their daily lives, without being asked. She is currently in a state of personal and professional transition, having undergone powerful transformation as a result of three years of cultivating a deep and earnest meditation practice.

"My practice is a conglomeration of some of the principles from Whole Heart Connection teachings of Thea Elijah, along with excerpts I've adapted from meditation practices that have evolved over thousands of years. What guides me at this point is the overpowering sense of peace I get when I do my practice. And on the days that I don't, there is an increased level of stress and general 'yuck' that permeates my speech and actions with myself and others."

Jeanette shares how her practice began, and how she does her meditation today. "A few years ago, I forced myself to do a three to five minute daily meditation, having the knowledge of how it was helpful to relieve blood pressure, stress and so many other health benefits we've all read in magazines. Today, I can easily sit for twenty to sixty minutes. I never would have thought this possible. I sit cross legged in a chair in my living room, close my eyes, and begin to focus on feeling grounded, connected to Mother Earth, breathing with awareness of the air coming into my nostrils, filling my lungs, filling me with Love and Light. Several inspirational books are kept next to my meditation chair. Selecting one of them, I find there's always a 'perfect' writing that addresses a message I need to hear for the day. Funny how the Universe works that way. Closing my eyes, I refocus on a light source that moves from my back through to the front of my body, moving through skin, connective tissue, bones, muscles, and ligaments. I breathe deeply and fill my entire human form with this Energy. Staying focused on this sensation of being filled with Light and Love, I find I want to sit for longer and longer periods."

Meditation really started to make sense to Jeanette when life became integrated with her practice. Says Jeanette: "Where the rubber meets the road is incorporating this feeling into my daily life. At work, I feel like a Giant Walking Head, always thinking, problem-solving, analyzing, being anxious about daily deadlines on reports and productivity. It's so easy to forget 'I'm a child of a Universal Love that is so far beyond my comprehension in its Magnificence.' It's so easy to forget there is something so much greater than me and my little tiny, insignificant ego (I'm upset because my latte order wasn't filled fast enough? Really?)"

The way Jeanette talks about her work mirrors the way parents talk about their daily life, reminding us that we are all in a relationship to our lives as a compassionate parent is to a beloved child. "My daily meditation sets the stage for my perspective for the whole day. My relationship with my boss is better, and the way in which I seek my next job, which will have something to do with children, will be more mindful. Before this practice I would have been snappy with my comments and responses with my boss, and inwardly defensive, self-loathing, and angry. Our relationship is still not great. I can't control her behavior, but with mindful communication, I can work with her and not let things build up and stew inside. Through meditation I have a tool of kindness that is much gentler on her and me alike."

Jerome and Nikki: Synergy

Jerome and Nikki are a young, recently married couple with a two-year old son, Liam. Jerome is a full time student in social work, and Nikki works as a registered nurse in the oncology ward at a VA hospital. They come from different backgrounds and mindfulness practices, but have found that their mutual love and support of one another work synergistically, and each also admires how their individual practices work together to help them parent Liam.

Jerome discovered about eight years ago—through an unexpected heart opening—that Zen meditation was his resonant path for navigating through life's challenges and relating to others. "I didn't know much about Eastern philosophy. But I was into physics, and read the Tao of Physics. My late teens and twenties were marked with tough times and mistakes. But through those, I started to ask questions, to look for deeper meanings. I looked into existentialism, physics, philosophy—what is this place that's great but can really be rough sometimes? I read an article on the holographic principle, about how particle physicists are finding new information on our universe to help us find answers to deep questions that don't have answers. I had a sudden opening experience during this time, and it was while I was taking a philosophy class. It led me to go right up to the professor and ask him: 'Are we the same?' He smiled, and as it turns out he was a Zen teacher and led a sitting group. I immediately became involved, and started sitting with his group and other meditation groups regularly.

"I didn't appreciate the sangha portion of it at first. After sitting with groups for awhile, I started sitting regularly on my own for two or three years. I was practicing every day; it was the most important thing in my life. In Zen, the teacher/student relationship is emphasized a lot because it is really good to have guidance. I didn't have guidance for those three years. I was in a cloud—happy, content, and off the ground, and it was wonderful. I was everything, blah blah blah. But it wasn't the complete way, which I soon found out.

"Nikki and I met in 2010, right around the time when many things started happening. I had started getting severe daily chest pains, and I could no longer work out at the gym every day. That really pulled me back to earth. The most difficult five years of my life followed. I slowly stopped my meditation practice as life got tough. Once you stop practicing it falls away—you look at your mat every day and that's about it. For two years it was like that. Doctors thought I had heart disease and was taking all kinds of medicines. Without Nikki, it would have been unbearable."

Jerome still kept trying to meditate, thinking it would help him through his pain. "Every couple of weeks, I would try to sit, but I never got any momentum to keep it going. If I hadn't had that opening from those earlier years or seen the benefits of meditation, I wouldn't have known that the pain in my body wasn't the only story. Just knowing that, and with Nikki's support, I was able to keep my head above water."

When Liam was born, it was a particularly difficult time for Jerome not just physically, but emotionally: "It made everything even harder. I felt like I couldn't be the father I wanted to be. I can't lift him up and carry him around, can't make him laugh."

But Liam also became Jerome's impetus to re-commit to his meditation practice. "I can't imagine life without Liam, without being a good father. He is just amazing. And Liam made me get serious about meditating with a sangha. Two years ago, I took my precepts and did retreats once or twice each year. The chest pains made it hard to sit, but Liam definitely gave me the motivation to get back to the things that make me a better person. I've really been diligent this past several months."

Eventually, doctors discovered that Jerome has a chronic inflammatory condition in the cartilage in his sternum and ribs that can be managed easily with medication. And with his physical symptoms easing, he took the next step: "When our guiding teacher asked if there was anyone in our area willing to keep our sangha going, I knew it was the right thing for me to do." Today, Jerome and his friend Zhen co-direct the Gateless Gate Zen Center in Gainesville, Florida.

Nikki is very appreciative of the impact Jerome's path has had on their family. "I never meditated in my life, but I love the fact that he has this practice in his life and that Liam has it in *his* life—a dad practicing Zen—it is such a good practice. It's not judgmental, doesn't recruit people, it's just so good."

Nikki continues: "I don't follow anything organized, but I used to run all the time. My thing was running right before I met Jerome, because I saw someone else's life transformed by running. I got addicted to it and loved it; it was such an outlet. I stopped when I got pregnant because it was a difficult pregnancy. I was so tired and nauseous all the time, and it was hard enough just to get out of bed and off to work. I've just started back again recently, with a half marathon goal coming up in the fall."

Jerome, showing the same type of appreciation for Nikki's running practice as she does for his meditation practice, made a comparison between the effects of both. "She has a glow and is happier after running. I can tell when she hasn't been running. It's kind of a parallel with my own practice. I want her to run, because it makes her happy, and she wants me to meditate."

Nikki notes that things are getting into equilibrium now. "He's doing his meditation practice a lot now, and I am running again. We need to be the best we can be for Liam, to set the best examples that we can as parents. If I am not well, it's hard on everybody."

Recently, when Nikki was very stressed out about exams, Jerome asked her to meditate with him. "Nikki asked me to sit the day before her nursing exam, because I told her it would make her feel better. But sitting doesn't always make you feel better. Sometimes you feel worse. Sometimes you feel better, sometimes it's easy, sometimes it's hard. But it's always the right direction in the long run, so I do ask Nikki if she wants to sit with me sometimes, when I think it might help." Jerome asked her: "Am I too pushy about it?"

Nikki was very honest in her reply: "Sometimes when you ask too many times you need to stop at a certain point. First I need to reestablish my running. We are just getting back into balance, and I know running and how it helps. I'm not that practiced in meditation. But I will definitely be open to sitting more and learning meditation as things continue to get back in balance."

That sense of letting life unfold with love and compassion for one another is the practice itself, which Jerome and Nikki are embodying beyond labels such as "I'm a meditator" or "I'm a runner." Their sensitivity and love for each other and for Liam is their bonding motivation, as both Jerome and Nikki believe that the best parenting is by example.

Adds Jerome: "I used to ask myself: How can a parent teach mindfulness, loving kindness? Now I understand."

AFTERWORD

Human consciousness is an extraordinarily interdependent phenomenon. Remember the evil slime in "Ghostbusters 2?" It was the cumulative amalgamation of the angry energy of New York City. Amazingly, the Ghostbusters discovered that the anger could be radically and instantaneously transformed into joyful energy when exposed to the song "Your Love Is Lifting Me Higher and Higher." When the populace of New York sang along, the slime actually accomplished supernatural feats of strength to defeat evil once and for all. But inasmuch as some movies and programs have wonderful messages reflective of the power of meditation, today's popular media is mostly insidious. It foments the already depressed state of the world's ills, violence, greed, and suffering with sensationalism and inanity at best, and outright fear mongering and brainwashing at worst. Because our consciousness is collective, 98% of the human population digests and manifests this garbage and lets it infect our daily lives. We have an epidemic on our hands.

Thankfully, just as the ills of the world are compounded by false media and corruption, meditation compounds our natural states of peace, joy, and the flow of effortless resolution. Your meditation infiltrates the stream of human consciousness, radically transforming the "slime." The effect you will have on others by dedicating yourself to this practice is profound. When you watch the news, when you feel fear for your children's safety because of the state of the world, when you see habitats destroyed or crimes of hate or injustice occurring too often, when you see others around you falling into stress or despair or illness, or when you are simply stressed out and overtired, there are many things you can do about it from a state of mindfulness. The first thing to do will be to lower your lids, without closing your eyes. Do not indulge your feelings. Do not push them away. Do not be pulled out into the "woe is me" of the mind. See. Relax. Feel. Allow. Breathe.

Ask "Who's Watching? Who's Feeling?" Breathe again. Notice the simple miracle of your breath. Accept all that comes through you. Keep breathing. Your kids are breathing with you. The world is breathing with you, and all are receiving the deep nourishment of your pure intention. Do-ership will follow, and it will come from a pure heart, aka Love, and this moment will be transformed.

Recently, I was cooking with my children and my young son noticed a bunch of bananas on the kitchen counter. "They were green yesterday, Mommy," he observed, "but now they're yellow. Maybe tomorrow we can make banana bread, when they are brown." His words hit my most inner being, as I suddenly perceived him in his greenness, my pre-teen daughter turning yellow, and then me, getting very brown and spotted, almost ready to be banana bread. This sense of impermanence brought tears to my eyes, and the moment was never sweeter. I loved his perception that the end of the cycle could be something as sweet and satisfying and totally purposeful as banana bread. No beginning, no end. Just the flow of life with love and gratitude for every stage which, through meditation, becomes your default intention.

Ultimately, this intention will permeate every aspect of your parenting experience, whether you are on the meditation cushion or not, and beyond. Thanks for sharing this practice, together.

Bows.

Poems

By Shana Smith

One of the seeker's greatest questions, and certainly one expressed at times by the hard-working parent, is: "If I am whole and complete, if I am Love embodied as the teachings say, then why do I feel so much pain?

CALL OF THE SUFFERING SOUL

Call:

Heaven, where art thou?
The sages tell me you are Now.
But Now is wracked, filled with pain
Pain in my body, in my brain.
Now is wrought with habitual fear
How can Heaven be so near?
For if that is all this moment contains,
Heaven, you have much to explain.

Response:

Stop. Dear soul, what is this?
There's nothing to solve, nothing to fix.
For the rain that pours on your parade
Brings forth the sun, grows trees for shade.
Problems arise and then they go
But they'll move right in should you indulge them so.
So breathe in this Now, so profound;
And Heaven in this moment will be found.

As busy as we may get, the simple act of the breath brings us into wordless connection with all existence.

ONE

The cool of this late summer morning
Has erased all but one knowing:
The Earth is exhaling again
And I am invited, with earnestness like a lover,
To breathe.

So often we hear the term "still the mind." But a parent's mind is never still. In addition to lists and chores and things to manage, we also enjoy the same ranges of highs and lows as any other living being. The essence of a parent's mind got me to perceive the word "still" in a different light, in every breath we take, to wit:

STILL

Autumn Rain: air heavy, wet, and sad
Soft cold shards soaking fragile skin
Yet still we must breathe through it
Until the rains clear, until the mists rise
Until the breath flows strong and free
Still.
Heart's Pain: tears heavy, wet, and sad
Soft warm daggers piercing fragile skin
Yet still we must breathe through it
Until the tears dry
Until the heart rises, the soul sings strong and free
Still we must breathe through it; Still we must breathe
Still.

We are all each other's teachers, and the way we live our lives is our curriculum.

THE SEEKER AND THE MOTHER

"Teach me the Way of the Buddha," said the young seeker. "Sure," I responded, then turned away to answer my toddler's cries. After returning to her, she repeated her question. "Teach me the Way of the Buddha." "My pleasure," I responded, then got up to change the baby's diaper. "Teach me the Way of the Buddha," she said again when I came back, this time with some exasperation in her voice. "One moment," I replied, then got up to shush the barking dog and serve lunch to the hungry children. When I returned to the cushion, she asked: "Are you ever going to have time to Teach me the Way of the Buddha?" "Yes. I enjoyed it very much; thank you! Gotta go now, and pick up my daughter from soccer. Gasshos." We bowed happily to one another.

My kids remind me of my own true nature and of the gift of each moment constantly, just in the way they experience life's wonders.

GIDDY NOW

Like a child about to get an ice cream cone,
Tingly, giddy, anticipating
Mouth watering, hands twitching, grasping, mouth laughing
So do I tingle and laugh
Now tasting the awareness of Suchness
Now filled with the sweet treat of Emptiness
Giddy in the light of knowing
Cherishing this life Now.

At the end of a recent weekend sesshin with my Zen teacher, Roshi Valerie Forstman, the traditional closing drum elicited a beautiful and profound sensation.

CLOSING DRUM

As each beat
Breaks into its smaller parts
Until it is but a fluttering of endless vibration,
So do I,
Whole and vast and complete
Break down, down
Pore by pore
Cell by cell
Into a Universe of infinitesimal pieces
Indelibly vast
In this moment
And the next.

Sometimes songs, well-rhymed, double as neat poems.

WE ARE ALL THE DIVINE MOTHER

We are all the Divine Mother
On a path back to ourselves we discover
That the Love that we know
Is from a Source that flows
From Beyond, and into each other.

We are all the light of Spirit
And if it calls out, we surely hear it
And the Love that unfurls
Is enough to change the world
As others heed this call, so they endear it.

We are all the enlightened Soul
We are pure, complete and free and whole
And so much Love does come
When we turn toward the One
When we walk the path of the masters long ago.

As the director of a meditation and yoga based retreat center, I often enjoy retreats on the sidelines, catching a sit, class, or dharma talk between organizing, cooking food for, cleaning up after, and hosting retreats. We recently had a week-long vipassana retreat with Steve Armstrong[xxxi], a wonderful teacher renowned worldwide for presenting the dharma as a way for living with an "unshakeable sense of well-being" and a "deeply happy life." The spirit of his teachings infused all of my chores and duties such that I was actively practicing meditation, as this poem reports:

PREPARING BREAKFAST FOR NOBLE FRIENDS

They sit on cushions
I sit on my thoughts, cutting fruit
One strawberry after another
They chant "Buddham Saranam Gachami."
Every note tumbles playfully out with the washing water
To carve the blade across the red skin and tiny seeds
Every note a reminder of miraculous presence.
Every note a reminder of Only. This. Happy. Strawberry.

Chores are endless. But really, it's just a matter of perspective.

THE TRASH CAN

Overfull
Unemptied
Spilling out onto the floor
Glaring at me
Waiting, waiting
For my statement,
My admonishment,
My punishment,
My declaration,
My busy-ness,
My purpose.
Glaring back, I see it change.
Whose trash can
Is too full?

I spent many years singing in beach bars and other venues. Learned a whole lot of songs that other people, usually semi-drunken, wanted to hear, so that I could squeeze in a few of my own. To this day, I still find myself drawn to the lone singer/songwriter set up outside amidst the clamoring crowds and clinking glasses, but why?

ONE LOVE

It begins with a song
Usually Baez, or Joni or JT
Voice strong and soaring over a gentle rhythm guitar
Reaching my ears just audibly enough that my head lifts and turns
To hear the tinkling applause
Nostrils catch the faint scents of cigars, swill, seafood and and swag
Head cranes and strains to hear the familiar set list:
Sam, Dave, Brown, Young, Simon, Garfunkel
Then a joke... laughs... irresistible laughs
The same laughs, the same songs, and yet
Like a magnet I am pulled
To the same deck, the same guitars
The same melting ice cubes in the same glasses
The same requests, the same tip jar
The same drunken fool asking for a Free Bird
The same ridiculously talented singer
Who tries to sing the same original masterpieces
Between Buffett and banter and Dylan and Marley
While the wild black ocean gurgles behind her
Behind the sun crisped tourists spilling brew and burgers onto the sand
Behind the piles of cigarillo butts and plastic wrappers rolling down the
shore
Singing songs too deep to get drunk to
Too personal to request
And tonight, caught in this trance,

I walk blindly towards the Voice, the Song
My own Voice, my Guitar, my masterpieces are here too
And the wild swamp behind the revelry waits for me, patiently,
Like the ocean always did
Warm and wild, pulsing with my very blood, humming with Infinity
And for the first time, I ask: "Is it you, Earth, I am hearing, you I am
singing for?"
Is your song the one I am always yearning to sing, yearning to hear
Yearning, drawing me back again and again
To the same melting ice cubes, the same drunken fools?
And, as always, it says: "yes."
And this time, I heard
While the leaves fluttered their applause.

The Chant of Boundless Compassion, which celebrates the awakening of Buddha-nature with the everyday sounds of the world, rings especially true with the sounds of Mother Earth. In the forest where we live, even while running around from one activity to the next, the birds are always calling me Home.

SPIRIT BIRDS

5:30am.
After a restless Night of dark dreams and fears
There cries a lone Owl outside my window, asking:
"Who? Shana, Who?"
Who is dreaming? Who is awakened?
Who hears, feels, cries, knows?
Who falls? Who rises?
Who cries now? Who is wholly being?
6:30am.
Flocks of spring birds guffaw and sing
Noisier than the alarm
Louder than the brooding of my insidious brain
"Up up up! No time to brood!
Up up up! We are here! Now!
You are here! Now!
Up! Up! Up!
7:30am
Red couch in the quiet of early morning
Tea in hand.
Heart swells, mind reacts, and I am caught in its pain again
Till a great hawk swoops in front of the window
Greatly interested in the morning bugs
But he lingers for me, stops my mind
So I am only Him.
He speaks for the owl, the birds, the trees, the dawn:

"Who? Shana, Who?"
Who is sitting, who is sipping? Who is brooding?
Who is here now?
Up! Up! Up!
You are here! Now! With me!
I love you.

When we are caught in repetitive roles day in and day out, such as mother, girlfriend, worker, husband, doctor, teacher, etc., it's good to remember that we are not our labels, but something much, much bigger.

SOAKED

Caught, again, succumbing
To the role of haggard mother
Slightly disheveled, lips pursed
Brow furrowed, shoulders hunched
Preparing, cleaning, organizing, chastising, praising
Supervising, sympathizing, serving, playing, sighing, loving
Remembering: this voice sings as strongly;
This body dances as fluidly
These eyes emanate as wildly
As the tortured artist,
The creatively insane,
The poetically genius,
The passionately expressive...
These same tired feet
This same weathered skin
This same longing heart
This same earnest soul
Surrendered and free as a hummingbird
Soaked to the feathers in an afternoon storm
Saturated in an ocean
Without air
Finally understanding
How to breathe.

I recently had a remarkable experience in which something didn't happen that I really, really wanted to happen. The pain and disappointment were so palpable that I was taken aback, because for whatever reason, not getting what I wanted brought back memories and emotions from past traumas, or "samskaras," dating all the way to childhood. But thanks to this practice, I was able to utilize those tremendously uncomfortable feelings for personal transformation. Not easy, but worth every inch of the process: so much better to suffer briefly, do this practice, and grow, rather than be stuck in a cycle of chronic and directionless suffering.

RELEASE

All-consuming becomes "woe-is-me,"
Eating you from the insides
Conspiring
To steal compassion from your marrow
To shine your bones dry and brittle
To mire you in the unmet wants
Of an insatiable, hungry fool.
To hold on
To hold on
To hold on
And to ask others, shamelessly, to hold on with you
Rather than seeing them just as they are
Knowing them, holding their space
In the light of love.
If you are to be burned by the flames of suffering,
As all who walk this green earth will be,
Be devoured completely.
Don't hold on to smoke and vapors
With white, desperate knuckles.
Don't dance around the coals of the cookfire
Crying over the scars of your little foot burns

Making sure everyone sees.
Bow to the pain and flames
Jump in, full bore
Call to the stars and moon as you burn, burn
Be consumed to ashes and dust
And wait, just wait
For soon you will open your palms freely
Letting golden rose petals float away
Wafting infinite scents of joy
Bounding in the pure freedom of this.
Just this.
All this.
And where agony once lived,
Will now rest only a smile, and deep, love-pooled eyes:
The face of the Universe.

REFERENCES

[i] http://greatergood.berkeley.edu/topic/mindfulness/definition

[ii] https://thebuddhistcentre.com/text/what-meditation

[iii] http://www.chopra.com/ccl-meditation/21dmc/meditation-tips.html

[iv] Reder, Alan. "Take a Seat" Yoga Journal
http://www.yogajournal.com/meditation/143_3.cfm

[v] http://www.sanbo-zen.org/sutras.pdf

[vi] His Holiness the XIV Dalai Lama, 1997. "The Four Noble Truths." Harper Collins Publishers, Hammersmith, London

[vii] Balsekar, Ramesh, 2009. "The End of Duality." Yogi Impressions Books, Mumbai, India

[viii] Singer, Michael, 2007. "The Untethered Soul: The Journey Beyond Yourself." New Harbinger Publications, Inc. Oakland, CA

[ix] Bikkhu Bodhi, 11/5/2014. "Purification of Mind." The Island, Upali Newspapers Ltd., Sri Lanka. Courtesy of Buddhist Publication Society

[x] Joko-Beck, Charlotte, 1994. "Nothing Special: Living Zen." Harper Collins, New York, NY

[xi] Yogananda, Paramahansa, 1946. "Autobiography of a Yogi." Self-Realization Fellowship, Los Angeles, CA

[xii] http://www.101zenstories.org/joshus-dog/

[xiii] His Holiness the XIV Dalai Lama, 1997. "The Four Noble Truths." Harper Collins Publishers, Hammersmith, London

[xiv] www.DennisMerrittJones.com

[xv] www.tou.org

[xvi] Garmon, Meredith, 2014. http://liberalpulpit.blogspot.com/

[xvii] Wolf, David B., 2012. "Relationships that Work: The Power of Conscious Living." Madala Publishing, San Rafael, CA

[xviii] www.Satvatove.com

[xix] Sasaki, Ruth Fuller, 2009. "The Record of Linji." University of Hawai'I Press, Honolulu, HI

[xx] Choose Again Society, www.choose-again.com

[xxi] Jai Maa, 2014. "Break Through Your Threshold: A Manual for Faith-Based Manifestation and Co-Creating with God." Independently Published.

[xxii] Rumi, Jelelludin. "The Guest House"

[xxiii] Hakuin's Song of Zazen

[xxiv] Brach, Tara, 2004. "Radical Acceptance: Embracing Your Life with the Heart of a Buddha." Bantam Dell, New York, NY

[xxv] Yogananda, Paramahansa, 1974. "Cosmic Chants." Self-Realization Fellowship, Los Angeles, CA

[xxvi] http://www.shinrin-yoku.org/

[xxvii] Stone, J. Tamar, 2011. "Selves In a Box"

xxviii Kanzeon Sutra, Translated by Hogen Bays. http://www.mkzc.org/kanzeon-sutra-mkzc-sangha/

xxix http://www.dalailama.com/teachings/training-the-mind/generating-themind-for-enlightenment

xxx Chant of Boundless Compassion, http://surrenderworks.com/Chant_of_Boundless_Compassion.html

xxxi www. http://www.dharmaseed.org/teacher/170/

About the Author

Shana Smith is a mom, musician, marine biologist, teacher, and writer. She is an avid and longtime practitioner of Zen and meditation, a decades-long yogi, and a much sought-after kirtaniya, or devotional chanting leader. Known across the state of Florida and the U.S. for the past 20 years as her award-winning children's entertainment persona "Shana Banana". Shana and her family (husband Dan, daughter Grace Ohana, and son Benny Albert) have settled down in Gainesville, Florida. From there they run the meditation and yoga-based Gainesville Retreat Center, which attracts many renowned teachers and practitioners. For more information, contact numbers and email, go to www.MeditationForMomsAndDads.com, www.GainesvilleRetreatCenter.com or www.ShanaBanana.com